THE CHILD'S BOOK
ON REPENTANCE

THE

CHILD'S BOOK

ON

REPENTANCE

Thomas H. Gallaudet

Solid Ground Christian Books
Birmingham, Alabama USA

Solid Ground Christian Books
2090 Columbiana Rd, Suite 2000
Birmingham, AL 35216
205-443-0311
sgcb@charter.net
http://solid-ground-books.com

The Child's Book on Repentance
WITH PRACTICAL ILLUSTRATIONS AND REMARKS

Thomas Hopkins Gallaudet (1787-1851)

Taken from 1834 edition by American Tract Society, New York

Solid Ground Classic Reprints

First printing of new edition September 2005

Cover work by Borgo Design, Tuscaloosa, AL
Contact them at nelbrown@comcast.net

CONTENTS.

Page.

Preface. 5

Address to Parents and Teachers. . . . 9

CHAP. 1.—Different kinds of sorrow. A person who repents, repents only of his own sins. . . 13

CHAP. 2.—What is sin? The impenitent, in the future
world, will think of their sins with deep sorrow.
Conscience. Free-agency. . . . 20

CHAP. 3.—Free-agency. Further explanation of what
sin is. Family happiness. A family must have a
head and laws. What is selfishness? . 27

CHAP. 4.—Further explanation of selfishness. Motives.
Evils of selfishness. It leads to resisting the authority of God. Breaking the laws of God is sin. 34

CHAP. 5.—Children of themselves discover some of the
laws of God, and break them. They may sin before they have any knowledge of God. Sin, if not
repented of, is always increasing. . . 41

CHAP. 6.—Recapitulation. Case of the thief in prison.
Sorrow for sin merely from fear of punishment is
not true repentance. 49

CHAP. 7.—Further illustrations of the same topic. Not
wrong to wish to escape future punishment. Case
of the poor boy's selfish sorrow. . . 56

CHAP. 8.—Confession of sin may be made, and its guilt
felt, without true repentance. True repentance
something more than a strong resolution to leave
off sinning, and to love and obey God. . . 65

CHAP. 9.—Repentance for one sin, if sincere, will be accompanied with repentance for all sins. Self-reproach. Case of Judas. . . . 73

Page

CHAP. 10.—Reparation may be made, and forgiveness implored, without true repentance. Recapitulation. 81

CHAP. 11.—True repentance leads to new views of God, and of his right to our entire love and obedience; to deep sorrow for ingratitude towards God; to new views of the laws of God, and of guilt in having broken them. 83

CHAP. 12.—The true penitent has new views of sin, as committed against God. He has a strong hatred of sin. He confesses his sins to God. He mourns over his guilt, in not having sought to do good to others. 94

CHAP. 13.—The true penitent mourns over his guilt, in having done wrong to others. He makes reparation. He mourns over his sins of thought and feelings, and longs to be pure in heart. He struggles against his peculiar sins. . . . 101

CHAP. 14.—The true penitent, in the strength of God, begins the work of an entire reformation. He lives and acts to be instrumental in leading others to Christ. 109

CHAP. 15.—He who begins to repent will keep on repenting. He will look to the Holy Spirit to aid and strengthen him in loving and serving God. He will rely entirely on what Christ did and suffered for forgiveness and acceptance with God. . 117

CHAP. 16.—How long does it take a person to repent? What keeps the sinner from repenting? . 125

CHAP. 17.—May the sinner pray for the Holy Spirit? How is it that the Holy Spirit leads the sinner to repentance, and yet that his repentance is his own act? The sinner urged to repent. . . 133

CHAP. 18.—Expostulation with the impenitent reader. 139

PREFACE.

In presenting another book to the notice of the religious public, the author would avail himself of the opportunity to make a few general remarks.

In doing this, he hopes so to gain the attention of parents, and teachers, and the friends of education, that, if their sentiments accord with his own, he may secure their influence and co-operation in a cause which lies very near his heart.

This cause is *the preparation of suitable religious books for children and youth!*

Many such, and most excellent in their kind, are already in circulation. But, with our rapidly increasing population, how many more will be needed.

Much improvement has of late years been made in this department of education, but there is room still for more.

The whole subject has not yet assumed its true importance in the minds of the religious public. More authors, whose experience and ability qualify them to write for children and youth, are greatly needed, and should be encouraged *to devote themselves to the work.* For it is only by *a course of practice* that skill is to be acquired, and improvements made, and excellence attained.

In order to bring forward such authors, and encourage them to persevere, parents, teachers, the friends of education, and Christians of intelligence and influence, must take a deeper interest in the subject. Clergymen generally, and those who occupy important stations in our literary and theological institutions, must take a deeper interest in it. Religious periodicals and reviews, although they have given it some considerable share of attention, must take a deeper interest in it.

But the inquiry will be made, " *How* is this deeper interest to be shown? Is there not already a good deal of it felt and manifested?"

That this is true there is no doubt. But in *one important particular* there is a great deficiency of this interest.

Very few, comparatively, of those who admit the immense importance to the interests of the Redeemer's kingdom of having suitable books prepared for the religious instruction of children and youth, *ever read these books*.

With regard to other subjects connected with the welfare of society and the advancement of knowledge and piety, we find that minds, even of *the highest order*, are patient in their investigations, and make a thorough analysis, and become acquainted with *the minutest particulars*. Indeed they are hardly willing to suffer the imputation of not possessing this knowledge of particulars.

Have not *books for children and youth*, constituting, as they do, *a mighty moral engine*, which is operating, and yet to operate with increased power, upon the temporal and eternal condition of the whole human family, have they not *equal claims* to be regarded with the deepest interest and attention ?

Why has science achieved such wonders by its application to the arts?

It is because minds of the first order have patiently and laboriously investigated its principles, and then tested their results by a careful *course of experiments* with the objects to which these principles were to be applied.

The science of mind and the science of language have *their peculiar principles*. How shall these principles be successfully applied to the cultivation of the youthful intellect and heart, through *the medium of books*, and important results be obtained, if *an equal share of attention*, on the part of the talented, the pious, and the influential, is not bestowed?

Is it not time to urge upon *such individuals* the duty of taking a deeper interest in this subject? Will they not be persuaded to form a correct opinion of the books prepared for children and youth, by *a careful perusal of them?*

They will thus become familiar with the operations of the youthful mind; they will learn what it requires; they will afford their aid in correcting the public taste so far as it may be wrong; they will be able to counsel and encourage authors; and in these and other ways give a new ardor to all who labor in the department of juvenile education, and especially to those who are concerned in carrying on one of the most important processes in this department, our Sabbath schools.

In reading books for *children and youth*, it will not be strange if those who are unaccustomed to teach them, should often grow impatient at the very slow and careful modes of explanation; at the continual going back to common and simple truths; at the humble comparisons taken from the most familiar objects; at *the drawing out* of thought, instead of expressing it concisely; and at the frequent repetitions.

But to form a proper estimate of all this, let a fair experiment be made.

Take a book written for children on some subject that requires *thinking* on their part, and sit down *with them*, to a careful perusal of it.

Propose questions to them, to see how far they understand what they are reading. Let these questions not be of that kind to which *yes*, or *no*, is the only answer. Let them not be such, that a reply can be formed merely by referring to the arrangement of the words and their construction into sentences. But let them be questions relating to *the general train of thought*, and to topics growing out of it. Let them be questions which will lead the little logician to the exercise of *his reflecting and reasoning powers*, and to the development of *his moral feelings*.

Invite questions on the part of the children, and see if the author furnishes a satisfactory answer. If not, attempt it yourself. Hear all their doubts and perplexities. Listen to their remarks, however strange they may seem and disconnected with the subject.

In short, *enter into their very thoughts and feelings* · and ascertain how far the author discovers an ability to do the same.

In this way some proper estimate can be formed of what *books for children and youth* ought to be; and of *the slow and careful analysis of thought and feeling* that should characterize them.

Will not *parents* at least make themselves acquainted with the books which are written for their children? Are not the immortal minds of their offspring worthy of this attention?

What an amount of deep and durable impressions these minds receive from the great variety of books with which they are so liberally furnished!

Are these books always what they ought to be? Are they intelligible, correct in sentiment, instructive, and useful?

How is it that parents who admit the solemn responsibility which rests upon them in the training up of their children for this and the future world, and who see book after book, engaging the attention of these *tender and susceptible minds,* and adding its powerful influence to the formation of their intellectual and moral character; how is it that they can neglect *to examine these books, and to ascertain the nature of this influence?* How is it that they can be satisfied with remaining ignorant of the character of *their children's most intimate companions and guides?*

ADDRESS

TO

PARENTS AND TEACHERS.

———————

THERE are many parents who love to teach their children about the Bible, and what they must do to obtain an interest in Jesus Christ, and secure the salvation of their souls.

Often such fathers and mothers spend an hour in the evening, or a portion of the Sabbath, in this delightful duty. And if they are faithful in the discharge of it, and in their prayers to God for his blessing, they have reason to hope that their labors will not be in vain.

Is there a father or mother who never does this, and whose eye may meet these pages?

What think you, my friends, of *the souls* of your children? Are they not entrusted to your care? Are they not receiving impressions from you, which neither time nor eternity will remove? What will be the consequence of your saying nothing to them on *the most important of all subjects?* Will *they* not, also, be led to treat it with neglect? What estimate will they form of God and the Savior; of death and the judgment; of heaven and of hell; if you never converse with them on these topics, nor show the interest that a parent ought to feel in them?

What account will you render for such neglect,

when you meet your children at the bar of God? O! the awful recollections, and *the fearful looking for of judgment*, which will then overwhelm the souls of the father and mother who have let their little ones grow up around them, and told them nothing of what *they must do to be saved!*

But you say you wish to discharge this duty, but do not know how to set about it.

Begin! Begin! Begin with *your own heart*. That must be right first. *Is it right with God?* Have you truly repented of sin, and trusted in the Lord Jesus Christ? Do you desire to imitate his example, and to be engaged in his service?

If you have none of these feelings, it is no wonder that you neglect the souls of your children! Will you any longer thus go on in the way to ruin, and give all the influence of your conduct to lead *them* with you? Become yourselves the friends of God and of the Redeemer, and you will soon find it both easy and pleasant to teach your offspring *their duty*.

To aid parents in thus devoting a portion of their time to the religious instruction of their children, was one of the objects which the author had in view in writing this book.

A father or mother can give a child a chapter in it to read attentively, and afterwards propose questions, to see if it is understood and recollected.

Or the book can be read by the parents to the children, at successive portions of time, to supply the place of conversation; and in some cases, perhaps, to lead to the more easy performance of this duty.

Does not the subject also deserve the regard of those who take an interest in Sabbath schools, or who are engaged in them as teachers?

How can the instruction which is given in these schools be considered thorough and effectual, until *some such analysis* of the leading doctrines of the Gospel, as is attempted in this book, forms a prominent part of it ?

The children, again and again, hear the duty *of repentance and faith* urged upon them. Unless they have *the meaning of these terms explained* in a way which is suited to their capacity—not by formal definitions, or by synonymous expressions,—but by going back to *simple, elementary truths*, and by illustrations, drawn from objects and events with which they are familiar,—how can they feel as they ought the obligations which are thus pressed upon them in the most solemn and affectionate manner ?

Is it not vastly important, also, that children and youth should early be accustomed to regard religious truth as deserving their fixed and patient attention, their close and continued thinking ? They must be trained to these *habits of mind* in the first stages of their education, or they will be in great danger of never having them afterwards.

They must make religious truth *a study.* They are required *to study* their lessons in the various branches of human knowledge to which they are attending ; to apply to them all the energy of their minds ; to learn them thoroughly and recite them accurately ; and to review them till they have made a durable impression on the memory. But *religious truth* can be gathered wholly from entertaining narratives and fictitious stories in a pleasant and captivating way ! No method, no demand for close and continued thinking, no study are necessary ! What an inconsistency !

Some parts of this book will, no doubt, be considered

by many parents and children as very dry and uninteresting. This is just what the author expects. *The
eleventh and twelfth chapters* will, probably, be the most
found fault with in this respect; and yet these are
the very chapters which ought to be the most attentively read, and carefully studied and reviewed.

The momentous subject of *repentance towards God,
and faith in the Lord Jesus Christ*—involving the
eternal destiny of the soul—cannot be made matter of
mere entertainment, even for children. They must be
taught to regard it as a very serious and solemn subject. How can they be led thoroughly to understand
it, and deeply to feel it, without great attention and
fixed application of mind, both on their part and on
the part of those who undertake to instruct them?

If any parents or teachers do not agree with the
author in these sentiments, he has but little hope of
their making this volume useful to the children entrusted to their care. Possibly, however, their perusal
of it may lead to a change in their sentiments.

To conclude, the book was written to be studied, and
reviewed and recited by children of a suitable age, *to
establish in their minds* correct and abiding views of
one of the fundamental doctrines of the Gospel.

THE CHILD'S BOOK,

ON REPENTANCE.

CHAPTER I.

1. Different kinds of sorrow. A person who repents, repents only of his own sins.

My young friends who read this book, or have it
read to them, may wish to know why I make it con-
sist of a number of conversations between a mother
and her children.

I do this that the subject may be more interesting.
I think, also, that in this way I can make it easier
to be understood.

We will suppose, then, that a pious woman, who
prayed much for her children, and with them also,
and desired to have them all the friends and fol
lowers of Jesus Christ, was seated with them, on a
Sabbath evening, round a cheerful fireside; and that
they had the following conversation.

Before they begin, however, we will give them all
names There was the mother, Mrs. Dormer; Wil

liam, twelve years of age; Eliza, nine; and Edward, six.

She used to encourage her children to talk with her very freely; and they did so, because they knew how much she loved them, and wished to have them gain useful knowledge.

It was Edward, the youngest, who began.

"Mother," said he, " I do not know that I understand exactly what it is *to repent of sin*. Will you please explain it to me?"

Mother. Yes, my son; and although I have talked with you all a good deal about it, I have been thinking, of late, that I ought to take more time and pains in enabling you to understand, clearly and fully, what it means.

Eliza. I know what it means, mother. It means *to be sorry for our sins.*

William. We all know *that*, sister. But I am glad that Edward asked mother about it; for I must say I often feel as if I had not yet understood *all* that it means.

Mother. Ah! my children, to understand, and *to feel*, all that it means, is no easy matter. The oldest and the most pious persons will tell you so. We need *the Holy Spirit* to teach us to understand and to feel what *true repentance is*. And while I am endeavoring to explain it to you, I beseech Almighty

God, for Christ's sake, to give you the Holy Spirit, that you may have the surest and best knowledge of what repentance is, *by feeling it in your hearts.*

You were right, Eliza, in saying that it means *to be sorry for our sins.*

But you all know there are many *different kinds of sorrow.* We must feel the *right kind* of sorrow for our sins; otherwise it cannot be said that *we repent of them.*

Eliza. You remember, mother, how sorry I was when it rained last Saturday, and kept us from taking the walk which you had promised us.

Edward. And how sorry I was when I lost my ball that uncle Robert gave me.

Mother. Well, let us talk a little about some of the different kinds of sorrow, and see what they are.

Was any body to blame, Eliza, that we could not take the walk last Saturday?

Eliza. No, mother. It was God who made it rain. And I remember you told us at the time that we ought not to fret or complain; because God gives us just such kind of weather as he thinks best, and that whatever he does is good and right.

Mother. We may be sorry, then, and wish that something had been different from what it was, when neither ourselves nor any one else had done any thing wrong.

William. I felt this kind of sorrow, mother, at the time that Edward was sliding on the ice and fell down and hurt himself so much. You gave him leave to go. He was doing nothing wrong. It made me feel very sorry to see the pain which he suffered, and I wished that he had not hurt himself.

Mother. Can any one of you give me another in-stance of this kind of sorrow?

Edward. I felt sorry, too, when I fell down on the ice. It makes me feel a little sorry now to think of it. I do not think I was ever so badly hurt be-fore in all my life.

Mother. Suppose, Edward, I had forbidden you to go and play on the ice, how would you have felt then?

Edward. I think, after I had got over the pain, and while brother William was leading me home, I should have felt sorry *because I had disobeyed you.*

Mother. Why would this have made you feel sorry?

Edward. Because I should have been afraid that you would punish me.

Mother. It seems, then, that there is another kind of sorrow. *It is the sorrow which we feel when we have done wrong, and when we suffer something, or expect to suffer something, because we have done wrong.*

William. I think, mother, that I feel sorry some times, not because I have done wrong *myself*, but because I see the children do wrong, and know that it will displease you.

Eliza. Yes; and you scold us about it, as if you were mother yourself.

Mother. My daughter, you do not speak properly to your brother. He is older than you and Edward; and if he reproves you when you do wrong, and I am not with you, he does right—though he should do it kindly. I am glad to see that any one of my children feels sorry when the others do wrong. *We should always feel sorry when we see any one doing wrong, and endeavor to show the person that he ought not to do it.*

This may be considered as still another kind of sorrow.

Do we not feel sorry sometimes because we have neglected to do what we ought to have done?

Eliza. O yes, mother! I remember last week when you went to take a walk, you told me to be a good girl, and sit still and study my Sabbath school lesson. I did not do it, and disobeyed you; and before you came home I began to feel sorry about it; but it was too late to get the lesson.

Edward. And *I* felt sorry one day that I did not mind you, mother, and stop making a noise when

William was sick. You remember you took my little wagon away from me, and would not let me have it again for three days; *that* made me feel very sorry.

Mother. And why did *you* feel sorry, Eliza, when you disobeyed me, and did not get your Sabbath school lesson?

Eliza. You know, mother. You told me that if I did not get it I should not take a ride with you the next day, and I was foolish enough to lose that beautiful ride for the sake of a little play.

Mother. We may speak, then, of another kind of sorrow. *It is the sorrow which we feel because we have neglected to do what we ought to have done, (or, in other words, because we have not done our duty,) and are suffering something, or expecting to suffer something, on that account.*

William. And I suppose, mother, *we can feel sorry at seeing others neglect to do their duty, just as we can feel sorry at seeing them do something wrong.*

Mother. Certainly, my son; and this may be considered as *one more kind of sorrow.*

We should not forget, at the same time, that it is *our duty*, in all proper ways, to endeavor to persuade others to do *their duty.*

Eliza. Mother, are any of the kinds of sorrow

that we have been talking about, the same that we must feel when we repent?

Mother. We may be sure that *some* of them are not. A person who repents, repents only of *his own sins.* He cannot repent of another person's sins. He may *feel sorry* that others have done wrong, or neglected to do their duty; but this is not what is meant by repentance.

God requires you to repent, because *you,*—you William—you, Eliza—you, Edward—have *yourself* done what is wrong, and also neglected to do *your duty.*

Neither do we say that we repent of any thing, for doing which, or for not doing which, *we were not to blame.*

We may *feel sorry* for it, but we do not say that we repent of it.

You remember that, yesterday, William, as he opened the door, pushed the handle of the lock against Edward's head, and hurt him so that he cried. William was not to blame in doing this. He did not think that Edward was so near the door. He was very sorry for what he did; but it would not be proper to say that *he repented of it.*

So I did not know till this morning that Edward had been unwell during the night. If I had known it sooner, I should have felt it to be my duty to get up and go and take care of him. I feel sorry that I did not know about it at the time, and go to do something for him. *But I do not repent of this;* for I was not at all to blame. I had no reason to think that Edward was sick.

But we have talked enough on this subject at this time: to-morrow we will converse again about it.

William, bring me the Bible, and tell Mary to come in. It is time for our evening prayer.

CHAPTER II.

What is sin? The impenitent, in the future world, will think of their sins with deep sorrow.—Conscience.—Free agency.

THE next evening Mrs. Dormer and the children were again seated round the fire, and had another conversation about repentance. And I may as well tell my young readers, without repeating it at the beginning of each chapter, that these conversations were continued almost every evening, till Mrs. Dormer had finished what she had to say on this interesting subject.

Mother. I expect, my dear children, as we go on endeavoring to find out what true repentance is, that you will be very attentive to all that is said.

It may not amuse you as a story would, but it is vastly more important than any story can be. It is so, for one short and plain reason.

Without true repentance for your sins, felt in your heart and showed in your conduct, you can never go to heaven.

Edward. Have the angels, mother, who are in heaven, ever repented?

Mother. Of what should they repent, Edward? Do you not remember that I told you last evening, that a person can repent only of his own sins? The angels in heaven *never have sinned*, and therefore they cannot repent.

It is only of sin that we can repent,—of our own sin—of our not being holy, as God requires—of something that we have done, which *we ought not to have done*, or of something that we have not done, which *we ought to have done*.

Eliza. Mother, what is *sin?*

Mother. We will talk about that; for it will help us to understand better what true repentance is.

Look at my watch. It is nearly half an hour too fast. Yesterday it was as much too slow. It has gone wrong for a week, and I cannot tell what is the matter with it.

Edward. Mother, I think you had better let William carry it to the watchmaker's.

Mother. Suppose I have a talk with it *for going wrong,* and try to make it feel that it is its duty to go right.

Edward. How would that do any good, mother? The watch does not know what is right nor what is wrong.

Mother. That is true, my son, *it cannot think nor feel.* It has no soul. It is impossible to make it understand what it is to do right or to do wrong.

William. A dog seems often to *think* about different things; and we are sure that he has *feeling.* Does *he* know, mother, what is right and what is wrong? Can he repent of any thing which he has done?

Mother. I think not, William. You can make a dog understand that *he must not do* certain things, or that *he must do* certain other things, and that if he is disobedient he will be punished.

If a dog is whipped several times for worrying a cat that lives in the same house with him, he will, at last, cease to do it, and treat her kindly.

He feels *pain* when he is whipped. The *fear* of being whipped again keeps him from worrying the cat. But he has nothing like *sorrow* in remembering that he did it. He has no feeling that it was wrong, and that *he was to blame, and deserves punishment.*

And this is true of all the other animals. They are not able *to understand* what is right and what is wrong. In this respect they are wholly unlike men, and women, and children. You may try all you can to teach them ever so little of God or the Bible, and it is in vain. They know nothing of God or of duty, of heaven or of hell. *They cannot therefore sin*, and of course they cannot repent.

William. I never thought before, in the same way that I do now, how very different we are from the animals, in being able to know what is right and what is wrong!

Eliza. I should think, mother, that very wicked people would sometimes wish to be like a dog.

Mother. Why do you think so, my daughter?

Eliza. It makes one *feel so bad* to be sorry for having done wrong, that it seems to me those who have done some very, very wicked thing, would wish to be like an animal, that they may not feel that they are to blame.

Mother. Ah! my daughter, very wicked persons have wished so: but in vain. *Those who sin, must think of their sins.* If they find out ways of forgetting them in this world, it will not be so in the next. *There*, those who die without repenting of their sins and trusting in the Lord Jesus Christ, will think of all their sins, and of their folly and guilt in commit-

ting them. They will think of this *continually*.
They will think of it with *the most painful feelings*.
They will *look back* with shame and horror at what
they have done. They will *look forward* at what
they are to be, and to suffer, with unspeakable despair.

Think of these things, my dear children, and while
we go on in finding out more exactly what *sin is*, remember that *you are sinners*, that you cannot avoid
thinking of your sins, and that if you try to forget
them in this life, and never repent of them, you will
think of them after you die, with *a sorrow of soul* of
which you can now form no idea. You cannot think
how awful and painful it will be.

William said truly, that we are very different from
the animals, in being able to know what is right
and what is wrong. We are also very different from
them, in having a soul which is capable of being
made *miserable for ever by sin*, and of enduring the
most terrible sufferings. The animals can suffer
great *bodily pain*, and so can *we;* but the severest
bodily sufferings are nothing compared with what
the soul will suffer, if it goes into the future world
with its sins unrepented of and unforgiven!

It is God who has thus made you very different
from the animals. *He* has given you your soul. He
has made it capable of understanding what right and

wrong are, and of feeling happy when you do right, and unhappy when you do wrong.

This being able to know when you do right and when you do wrong, together with the *happy* feelings which you have when you look upon your right feelings and conduct, and the *unhappy* feelings which you have when you look upon your wrong feelings and conduct, may all be spoken of *in one word*, by saying that you have *a conscience.*

William. Have very little infants consciences mother ?

Mother. It is very difficult for us, my son, to tell *the exact time* when they first feel that they are doing right or doing wrong. They may have such feelings long before they show them *distinctly* in their conduct.

But it is not necessary for you or me to know all about *the consciences of infants.*

If I can make you understand *what your own conscience is,* and that you are a sinner in the sight of God; if I can explain to you what true repentance is, and lead you to feel it in your heart; if I can thus, with the aid of the Holy Spirit, show you your guilt and danger, and persuade you to trust in Christ as your only Savior; I shall care not at all whether I can answer such a question as William has just put me or not.

All such curious and difficult subjects I leave with God, who made the souls of little infants, and knows how to treat them with the greatest kindness and the most exact justice.

Eliza, when you disobeyed me in not getting your Sabbath school lesson, were you *obliged* to feel and to act so? Could you have felt and acted *differently*, and have been an obedient girl, and sit still, and learned your lesson?

Eliza. I suppose I could, mother, if I had *wished* to do so.

Mother. You did, then, *just as you chose to do;* or, in other words, you acted freely; or, what means the same thing, *you were a free agent.*

Edward. Am *I* a free agent too, mother?

Mother. Let us see whether you are. Go bring me that book.

[Edward carries the book to his mother.]

You have done as I told you. You have obeyed me, and been a good boy.

Could you have disobeyed me?

Edward. I suppose so, mother. There have been times when I disobeyed you; and if I had *chosen* to disobey you now, I could have done it.

Mother. If I should tell you, Edward, to fly up to the ceiling, could you do it?

Edward. No, mother; 'or I have no wings.

Mother. Would you feel that you were to blame for not doing it?

Edward. I should not.

Mother. If I should tell you to walk across the floor, and you should not do it, would you feel that you were to blame?

Edward. I should certainly feel so. I can *walk* if I choose; but I cannot *fly*, if I wish to do it ever so much.

Mother. You see then, my son, that you are a free agent in some things, but not in others.

To-morrow we will talk a little more about your being a free agent.

CHAPTER III.

Free-agency. Further explanation of what sin is. Family happiness. A family must have a head and laws. What is selfishness?

Mother. Well, my children, I see that you are all *free agents.* I told you this morning to meet me here at six o'clock, and you are very punctual. Have you been long here?

William. Only a few minutes, mother.

Mother. You might have staid away, and disobeyed me, if you had chosen to do so.

Edward. *I* wanted a little, mother, to stay away a short time, and look at the pictures that Mary was showing me.

Mother. Why did you not do so? You *could* have done so, if you had chosen to do it.

Edward. Yes, but I did *not* choose to do it.

Mother. Why did you not choose to stay with Mary rather than to come here?

Edward. I thought that you would be displeased with me, and that I should feel unhappy at disobeying you. Besides, I wished to hear you talk, though I wanted to look at the pictures too.

Mother. Just so you all often want to do something, and think at the same time that *you ought not to do it.* Or you wish *not* to do something, and yet think that *you ought to do it.*

Very soon *you choose* which of the *two things* you will do. If you do right, you feel *happy* in doing so, and you feel *unhappy* if you do wrong.

Eliza. How exactly you know, mother, about my feelings! I have felt just as you have been telling us hundreds of times.

William. So have I.

Edward. And *I* too, when I wanted to climb up the tree after the bird's nest, and knew I ought not, because mother had forbidden me.

Mother. Did you climb up the tree?

Edward. I did not, and I felt very glad afterwards that I did not disobey you.

Mother. You see, my children, that in a great many things you are free agents. You *know* what is *right* and what is *wrong*, and you can *do* either right or wrong, *as you choose.* Now, answer me one question.

When you have felt as you ought, and done right, and felt *happy* afterwards; or felt as you ought not, and done wrong, and felt *unhappy* afterwards; have you not felt and done *just as you chose?*

Children. Yes, yes, yes.

Mother. Did it seem to you as if any body or any thing were obliging or forcing you to feel and to do as you did?

William. No, mother; only sometimes it seems to me to be very difficult to feel and do as I ought.

Mother. What makes it so difficult?

William. That is a hard question, mother. When I feel like a good boy, and love you, and wish to please you, and love Eliza and Edward, and wish to do them good, it is very *easy* for me to do right. But sometimes I do not feel so. I want *to please myself;* I do not care at all about others; and then it is *very difficult* for me to do right.

Mother. Do you not feel that you are *to blame* when you feel so?

William. I do, and that makes me the more un-happy.

Mother. Well, my children, *you all know and feel that you are free agents.*

You understand, with regard to a great many things, what is right and what is wrong. If you feel and do right, you feel and do so *yourselves,* freely. If you feel and do wrong, you feel and do so *your-selves,* freely.

When you feel and do right, *your conscience ap-proves it,* and you are happy. When you feel and do wrong, *your conscience disapproves it,* and you are unhappy.

You see then that *you are sinners.* For you have felt and done wrong a great many, many times. You have felt and done as you *ought not to do;* and you have *not* felt and done as you *ought to do.*

Eliza. Is every body a sinner, mother?

Mother. Yes, my daughter, all, all have sinned, and need to repent of their sins, and to trust in Christ, that they may be pardoned and saved.

But I wish you, my children, not to think about others, but about yourselves. I wish you to think and *to feel* that *you* are sinners. For unless you do this, you will not repent of your sins, and trust in Christ for salvation.

William. I know that *I* have sinned, and that I

am to blame for it; but I wish, mother, to understand better than I do *what sin is.*

Mother. I was about to explain it more fully to you; and while I am doing it, I wish you all to be very attentive to what I am saying.

What do you think, William, would become of our little family, if I should let you, children, and Mary, do as you choose, and have no kind of government over you?

William. I know how it would be, mother. It would be as it was the day that you went to aunt Sarah's, when we had so much disputing, and confusion, and trouble.

Eliza. Well, William, it was all because you wanted to be master.

Edward. No, it was not, Eliza; for *you* began first, ordering Mary about, and William told you it was wrong to do so.

Mother. Be still, my children; you know I examined into your conduct when I came home, and the matter was all settled weeks ago. We do not want to have it brought up again. I am sorry that you have a disposition still to dispute about it. It shows, at this very time, how necessary it is *that the family should have a head,* and that I should govern it and keep it in order.

William. I am glad, mother, for one, that you govern us all. We should soon have trouble enough if you did not.

Mother. What would cause this trouble?

William. Just what caused it, mother, the day that you were gone. We should not agree together. One would want to do *one thing* and another *a different thing*. I am afraid each would wish to govern all the rest, and so there would be no order, but all would be in confusion.

Mother. And the true reason of this, my children, would be, that each would wish *to make himself or herself happy*, and care little or nothing about the happiness of the rest.

Suppose I should think all day long only how to make myself happy, and care nothing about your comfort and happiness, what would become of you all?

Edward. I don't think we should have any breakfast, or dinner, or supper pretty soon; and when my clothes got torn, who would mend them?

Eliza. Yes, and who would buy wood for us, and have it sawed, and split, and piled up in the woodhouse?

William. And who would send us to school, and get books for us, and teach us about the Bible?

Mother. Suppose, too, I should let each one of you do as you choose, and not require you to do that which is for the comfort and good of us all—*of the whole family.*

William. I am afraid, mother, we should be *a very different family* from what we now are.

Mother. Indeed we should. You would soon find out how necessary it is that each one in a family, in order to make it comfortable and happy, *must not be selfish.*

You would soon find out that each one must do that which will be for *the good of the whole.*

You would see, too, that if what any one thinks is for his or her *own particular good,* is not for the good of the whole, but interferes with it, it must be given up; and that if it is not given up willingly, the person *must be made* to give it up.

You would see that there must be government in a family, and rules or *laws,* to which all must submit; and *punishments,* too, for those who break the laws; and *a head,* to see that the laws are obeyed, and offenders punished, and the good order and happiness of the family preserved.

William. Mother, I never thought of all this before. I see now what a selfish and disobedient child I have often been, and how much trouble I must have given you by my misconduct.

Mother. I am glad to hear you say so, my son. I wish you could all see *and feel,* more than you do, both *the evil and the guilt of being selfish and dis-obedient.*

Edward. What is it, mother, to be selfish?

Mother. Do you remember that yesterday, when Eliza asked you for a piece of your apple, you would not give her any?

Edward. Well, she would not give me any of hers the day before.

Mother. Then you were both selfish, and you both know what it means to be so.

Whenever you wish to get something good for *your self alone*, or to seek your own comfort or enjoyment and do not wish and try, so far as you are able, *to do the same good to others*, and to make them as comfortable and happy as you are yourself, *you are selfish.*

You all know what I mean, but I will explain something more about it to you in our next conversation.

CHAPTER IV.

Farther explanation of selfishness. Motives. Evils of selfishness. It leads to resisting the authority of God. Breaking the laws of God is sin.

Mother. We were talking yesterday, my children, about selfishness. We will endeavor now to examine still farther what it is: for in this way we shall see more clearly what sin is.

William, do you not very often, when you say or do something, think at the time *why* you say or do it? Do you not wish, by saying or doing it, to get something *else*, either for yourself or others?

William. O yes, mother. When I worked so hard the other morning in piling up the wood, I thought all the time of what you told me. You said, if I got it done in one hour, that you would take me to ride with you. And the reason *why* I worked so hard was, that I wished to take that pleasant ride.

Mother. And, Eliza, *why* did you knit so fast on the stocking this afternoon?

Eliza. You told me, mother, that the poor little girl for whom I was knitting it would want it very soon, and I wished to get it done as soon as I could.

Mother. These reasons *why* we do certain things, or *why* we do not do certain things, are called *motives.*

If we can find out what our motives are when we say or do any thing, we can easily tell whether, in saying or doing it, we are selfish or not.

If our motives are only to get something good for ourselves, and if we have no wish, and try not at all to do good to others, we are selfish.

Eliza. But, mother, may we not seek *our own* comfort and happiness?

Mother. Certainly, my child. It is right that you should do so, if you seek that which will really make you happy—not happy just at the time, but continually and uniformly happy—not happy merely in this world, but happy for ever.

But if you seek your happiness in such a way as to interfere with the real good of others, or if you do not endeavor, so far as you are able, to have others get as much good and enjoy as much happiness as yourself, then you are selfish in your feelings and conduct.

William. The more you explain these things to us, mother, the more I fear that I have been a very selfish boy. I understand what is meant by motives; and when I think of my motives in what I have said and done, I must confess that I have cared but little about the good of others, and have sought almost entirely my own good alone.

Mother. Yes, my son, and I fear you have *always* done so; for I must be very plain with you, my children, and tell you that I cannot yet see, in any of you, a disposition like that which God requires us to have.

He says in the Bible, that *we must love others as we love ourselves.*

Ah! when will you feel this love, my dear children? When will you seek your true happiness in endeavoring to make others happy?

You have seen what evils selfishness would produce, even in our little family, if each one were left to do as he or she chose, and if there were no head, and no laws.

William. One day, mother, the master was absent two or three hours from school, and you cannot think what confusion and trouble we had there. It was a very cold day, and the boys were crowding round the stove, and pushing each other so hard that they almost came to blows; and some did this who did not wish to get near the fire, but only to make a noise.

Mother. Each one, my son, was seeking his own particular comfort, without any regard to that of others, or to the good of the whole. They were selfish in their motives and conduct, and some were acting wrong merely to gratify their sinful disposition and love of mischief.

Suppose all the people in our town were equally selfish, and that there were no laws to keep them in order. Suppose they were disputing and quarreling, as the boys did round the stove; each trying to get something to add to his own comfort and happiness, or to gratify his wicked disposition, and not caring, in doing this, how much he might make all the rest unhappy.

William. I should not wish to live in such a place; it would be a great deal worse than the school-room was when the master was absent.

Mother. Now think a little farther, my children. Suppose the same thing was true of all the people in the world. Suppose that no one was kept, by any fear of God or of man, from planning and acting from selfish and sinful motives—from endeavoring to make himself the greatest and the happiest—no matter how miserable, in doing this, he might render his fellow-men.

William. I can think, mother, how much confusion and misery there would be, from the trouble that we had, even in our small family, the day that you were absent.

Mother. But we must not stop here. The people that live in this world are a very small part of all the beings whom God has formed. How many other worlds there are which are full of inhabitants, God has not told us. Heaven, we know, is full of holy and happy beings, and hell of wicked and miserable ones. It is probable that there are thousands and millions of other beings besides, in other worlds.

Now suppose that all the beings who are in existence should be under the government of God no longer, and each be permitted to do as he pleased, without any fear of punishment. Suppose too, that each should be supremely selfish and sinful, having no regard to the good of others and to the welfare of the whole, nor caring how much he thus injured others. What universal and terrible misery there would be!

William. I am glad, indeed, that it is not so.

Mother. You have reason, my son, to be glad. You have reason to rejoice that God reigns; that he is at the head of all the beings whom he has formed; and that his laws are holy, just, and good.

In him there is no sinful disposition, no selfishness. He desires to make his creatures happy. He is continually showing us, in ten thousand ways, how good he is. The Bible tells us that *he is love.*

O how great was his love towards us in giving his only and well-beloved Son to die for us! And how great was the love of Jesus Christ to us, that he could come down from heaven, and lead a life of sorrow, and die a most cruel and shameful death, that he might save us from the punishment which our sins deserve!

When we consider this love of Christ, how mean, and hateful, and sinful, does our own selfishness appear! *We,* for whom Christ died, thinking only of the happiness of our own little self, and striving to promote our own good without regarding the good of others, and even willing that others should suffer, and greatly too, rather than make the least sacrifice or give up ever so little of our comfort and convenience, and what is worse than all, injuring others without promoting our own happiness.

It was this selfishness which caused so much unhappiness (as William has told us) in the family, the day that I was absent.

It is the same selfishness, my children, which has caused by far the greatest part of all the unhappiness which we have had in our family. It has been the source of your disputes and quarrels with each other. It has led you, at times, to feel unwilling to submit to my authority. It has led you to disobey me either in doing what I directed you *not to do*, or in not doing what I have commanded you *to do*.

Ah! it has led you to disobey a still higher authority than mine, even that of God himself. His will is, that you should seek the happiness of others as well as your own, that you should love others as you love yourself. All the commands which he has given us in the Bible, are holy, just, and good. It is right that he should rule over us. He made us, and gives us all our comforts, and blessings, and privileges. We owe him the entire obedience of our hearts, and of our lives.

He rules over us, too, for our own good, if we will love and obey him. His laws are made for the good of the beings whom he has formed. If we and all other beings would obey his laws, there would be happiness every where, constant and perfect.

But alas! my dear children, you have broken these

laws of God. Your selfishness has led you to do this, just as it has led you to break my commands.

This breaking of the laws of God, as he has given them to us in the Bible, or as they may be found out in any other way, is sin.

Remember that his two great laws, and which include all the rest, are, *Thou shalt love the Lord thy God with all thy heart, and with all thy soul, and with all thy strength, and with all thy mind, and thy neighbor as thyself.* Your selfish and sinful heart leads you to feel unwilling to submit to these laws, and to the others which are included in them. You refuse to submit to them; you disobey them; and all this is sin.

CHAPTER V.

Children of themselves discover some of the laws of God, and break them. They may sin before they have any knowledge of God. Sin, if not repented of, is always increasing.

William. You told us yesterday, mother, that our breaking the laws of God is sin.

Did I sin when I was a little child, and did not know any thing about God or his laws?

Mother. My son, God teaches us in the Bible *that*

you were born in sin; that you have gone astray, or *been a sinner from your earliest days; and that your heart, until it is renewed by the Holy Spirit, is deceitful above all things, and desperately wicked.*

Now, to show you that this is true, let me ask you all one question.

When you were very young children, and as far back as you can remember, did you not often feel that you were to blame?

William. I did, mother.

Eliza. And so did I.

Edward. And I too.

William. Still, mother, you told us that sin is *breaking the laws of God.* I do not yet see how we could sin, when we did not know any thing about these laws.

Mother. It is true that I said yesterday, "The breaking of the laws of God, as he has given them to us in the Bible, or *as they may be found out in any other way*, is sin."

These laws require that we should *be holy*, that is, that we should love God supremely, and obey him in all things, and love others as we do ourselves.

Now there are several ways in which God makes known to us his laws.

In the *Bible*, indeed, he has told us by far the most about himself, and what he requires us to be and to do ; and it is in that blessed book that we must principally gain the knowledge of his laws.

He shows himself to us also in *the things which he has made*, and which he governs by certain laws, many of which we can find out.

We have found out that the sun rises and sets at certain hours, and that summer and winter return at regular periods of time. We must attend to our business accordingly. If men should attempt to sleep all day, and work all night, and to plant seed only in the middle of winter, they would act not only foolishly but wickedly. It would be *sin in them* to disregard the laws of God in these respects, as well as the laws which he has given us in the Bible.

So if a person finds out that eating or drinking some particular thing is hurtful to him, that it is like a poison, injuring his health and strength, he has found out *a law of God* concerning that thing ; and f he continues to use it, he breaks this law of God, *ind sins against him*.

William. Is not that the reason, mother, why it is sinful to use spirituous liquors as a drink ?

Mother. Yes, my son, and I am glad that you understand so well what I have been saying. You have made a good application of it.

Eliza. Why is it a sin, mother, to use any thing that will injure our health or strength ?

Mother. If our body becomes sickly and feeble, our mind will be affected by it. We shall be the less able to love God *with our whole soul, and strength, and mind,* and to do good to others. We shall be the less able to do our duty in many respects.

So you see how breaking any one of the laws of God, whether it is taught us in the Bible, or whether we find it out in any other way, lead us to break other laws of his, or prevents us from obeying them as we ought.

And this is one of the great evils of sin. *The commission of one sin always prepares the way for the commission of other sins.* He who breaks one law of God, is often at the same time breaking other laws, or preparing soon to break them.

Some laws of God, even little children find out, without any one's teaching them.

They find out of themselves many things which are right and wrong. They soon begin to see that many things which they say and do can make others happy, or unhappy. *They feel that it is right* to make others happy, and *wrong* to make them unhappy.

They see a father and mother, older and wiser than themselves, at the head of the family. *They feel that it is right* that this father and mother should be obeyed, and that disobedience to them deserves punishment.

They see brothers and sisters around them; and *they feel that it is right* that they should love these brothers and sisters, and be kind to them, and treat them as they would be treated by them.

They feel that it is wrong not to act so towards their father and mother, and brothers and sisters.

Now it is God who gives children *minds* capable of finding out these things, and *hearts* capable of feeling them. In other words, he gives them *consciences.*

He also orders it so that children will certainly learn and feel these things, from what they see in themselves, and in others around them.

That they should thus learn and feel these things, may be considered as *laws of God.*

If children, then, act contrary to what *their consciences* say is right, they break the laws of God. They feel that they are to blame. *God has made them so that they feel guilty;* and in this way they may properly be said *to sin,* by breaking the laws of God, although they may not yet know any thing about God.

In doing this, they show *that wickedness of heart* which would lead them to break any law of God, if they could understand that he had actually given them the law, and if they should think that it interfered with their own comfort and enjoyment.

Edward. Mother, I am a little boy, but I know that what you say is true. I can remember thinking and feeling just as you say children do about what is right and what is wrong.

Mother. Yes, every child knows it. And he knows, too, that his father, and mother, and teacher, often explain to him what is right and what is wrong. And his conscience approves of what they say, although he may be so young that he has not yet learned much, if any thing, about God.

He sees that his father, and mother, and teacher, are *his superiors ; and he feels that it is right they should be obeyed.*

And if children disregard the instructions of parents and teachers, and do not obey them, they may properly be said *to sin* by breaking *the laws of God,* although they may not yet know much, if any thing, about God.

In doing this, they show *that opposition to rightful authority* which would be unwilling to yield to the authority of God himself, if it should interfere with their selfish wishes and desires.

You see, then, my children, that sin is just what we are told it is in the Bible, *a transgression of the law of God—an acting contrary to the law of God —the disobedience of it in our feelings and conduct, and not being and doing all that it requires.*

You see, also, that little children can sin, and *do sin*, even before they have learned any thing about God and the Bible. They very early show that the sin of Adam and Eve, which was the cause of bringing so much sin and misery into the world, has reached down to them. They very early show that their hearts have no love to God, or disposition to obey his laws; and that thus they are the sinful descendants of the sinful father and mother of the whole human family. They very early show that they have within them *that sinful disposition, and that selfishness and opposition to rightful authority*, which opposes the will of God, as expressed in his laws which he has given to us in the Bible. And this sinful disposition shows itself in opposition to *all the laws* of God just as soon as the child becomes acquainted with them; and continues thus to show itself until his heart is renewed by the Holy Spirit.

Edward. Mother, sin is a very bad thing. I never thought before that it was so bad.

Mother. What you say, Edward, is very true. Sin, even in little children, is a very bad thing. You know how much evil it causes. It makes them, and all around them, unhappy. It destroys the good order and comfort of families. It makes fathers and mothers weep over the misconduct of their children. It fills them with fear of what their children may become as they grow older.

Ah! this growing worse as they grow older is the most dreadful part of the sinfulness of young children.

Sin, if not repented of and overcome, is always increasing.

The little child who is obstinate and self-wi led, and refuses to obey the command of the parent, and does wrong things which the parent forbids it to do, unless a great change takes place in it, will go on to sin more and more. Its obstinacy and self-will will increase. It may live to become so hardened in sin as to despise the laws of God and of man, and to commit some dreadful crime, and even to suffer death as the punishment of its offence.

Besides this, think, my children, how displeased the great and holy God is with you when you sin.

In sinning, you break *his* laws and despise *his* authority. You show yourselves to be ungrateful to the Being who has been so kind to you, and who has loved you so much as to send his only and well-beloved Son into the world to die for you.

You show that you are opposed to what he is doing to make his creatures happy, that you care not for the happiness of others, and that you are unfit to go to that world where all are happy in loving and serving God, and in loving all around them.

Think of these things, my children; and may the

Holy Spirit lead you so to think and feel with regard to them, that what I have said may do you good.

CHAPTER VI.

Recapitulation. Case of the thief in prison. Sorrow for sin, merely from fear of punishment, is not true repentance.

William. Before you go on this evening, mother, to tell us any thing new, I should like very much to have you tell us over again, a little, some of the things which you have been teaching us.

Mother. That I will cheerfully do, my son; for I wish you all to understand clearly what sin is, that so you may understand what it is to repent of sin.

Give me then your fixed attention.

I have attempted to show you that you have wicked hearts, and that you are also free agents. You have *minds* capable of knowing what right is, and what wrong is. You have *hearts* capable of feeling happy when you do right, and unhappy when you do wrong. You have *consciences* which approve your conduct when you do right, and you feel happy; and which disapprove your conduct when you do wrong, and you feel unhappy. And in addition to all this, you feel within yourselves that nothing *forces* you to do right, or to do wrong; but that you do right or wrong *freely*, and exactly as you choose.

Now, God has not left you ignorant of what right and wrong are. He has taken great care to teach you what *his laws* are, with regard to right and wrong. He has so ordered it, that in many things you have found out yourselves what his laws are, what you ought to do, and what you ought not to do. He has also provided for you parents and teachers, who instruct you still further with regard to your duty. And that both they and you may know more clearly and fully what his will is, he has given us, in the Bible, more of his laws. By obeying these laws we shall take the surest way of making ourselves and others the most happy that we can be in this world, and of securing our everlasting happiness beyond the grave.

God made his laws, that he might let his creatures know his will, and see what a great, wise, good, holy and just Being he is, and that it is right and best that he should be *at the head* of all the beings and things that he has made.

God made his laws, that, by obeying them, his creatures may render to him that love and honor which are so justly due to him.

God made his laws, that, by obeying them, his creatures may be good and holy like himself.

God made his laws, that, by obeying them, his creatures may, each one of them, get the greatest happiness of which they are capable, both now and for ever.

God made his laws, that, by obeying them, his creatures may form *one great family of love;* all happy in loving and obeying the Father who made, and sustains, and blesses them; and in loving others, and seeing them good and happy.

God made his laws, that, if any of his creatures, notwithstanding all his kindness towards them, still refuse to obey these laws, he may show them, and all other beings, that his authority must be preserved.

For we have seen what confusion and misery would take place, if God should not govern all the beings whom he has made; if they should be permitted to submit to his authority, or not, as they choose.

God will preserve his authority. He will be just as well as good. He will show his terrible displeasure against all the beings *who are unwilling to obey his laws.* He will punish them in a most severe and awful manner, by banishing them, for ever, from his presence, and letting them suffer the wretchedness which their own conduct will both cause and deserve.

You see, my children, some of the reasons why God has given us laws.

These laws, like himself, are holy, just, and good. Your consciences approve of them. *You feel that you ought to obey them.*

Now, *the disobedience of these laws is sin.*

Men, women, and children disobey these laws of God, because they have *sinful and selfish hearts.* These laws are directly opposed to this sinfulness. They require that we should love God with our whole soul, and strength, and mind, and that we should love others as we love ourselves.

This interferes with the sinner's selfish desire to seek his own particular good in a way that would lessen or destroy the good of others. He has no regard to this good of others, to the good of *the great family of beings,* of which God is the father and head.

The sinner, therefore, dislikes these laws of God. He is unwilling to obey them. He refuses to submit to the just and good government of God.

If all these things are so, you cannot doubt, my children, that you are sinners.

You understand *why* you are sinners, and *how* you are sinners. And I hope this will lead you to take a deep interest in what we are to talk about, with regard to repenting of sin.

For it is of the greatest importance that you should know exactly what true repentance is, and that you should feel it in your hearts. It is important, because if sin is such an evil as we have seen it to be, you ought to desire, more than any thing else, to be freed from it. And God has assured us, in his word, that without repentance you can never be freed from sin.

We will now endeavor to find out what true repentance is; and in order to do this, I must remind you of some things which were said at our first conversation.

Eliza. What, mother, when we talked about the different kinds of sorrow?

Mother. Yes; and you all recollect two kinds of sorrow that were mentioned; one is that which we feel when we have done wrong, and when we suffer something, or expect to suffer something because we have done wrong; and *the other* is that which we feel because we have not done what we ought to have done, and suffer something, or expect to suffer something on that account.

Edward. You know the man, mother, who stole the money from uncle last spring. He is in prison now, and I think he must feel very sorry.

Mother. I dare say he does, my son. He feels sorry that he is confined, and that he has to work hard, and cannot talk with any body. Do you think that he feels sorry that he stole the money?

Edward. I should think that he does, for if he had not stolen it he would not be in prison.

Mother. Is it known whether he ever stole any money before?

William. I believe he has confessed that he did, a great many times; but he was never found out before.

Mother. Do you suppose, Edward, that he felt sorry after he had stolen any money, while he thought that it would not be found out?

Edward. I am not sure, mother, but I rather think he did not; for if he did, he would not have kept on stealing.

Mother. When he stole the money from your uncle, and it was found under the barn where he had been working, and he was suspected, and charged with having taken it, do you think he felt sorry?

Edward. I suppose he did, for then he began to fear that he might be sent to jail.

Mother. Did the sorrow which he felt at that time, or does the sorrow which you think he feels now, show, that he has felt that it is wrong to steal? Does it show that he is willing to tell your uncle that he did wickedly in stealing the money from him, and to ask his forgiveness?

Does it show that he is willing to ask the forgiveness of all from whom he has heretofore stolen, and to restore what he took from them, so far as it may be in his power to do it?

Does it show that he would not steal again if he had the opportunity, and thought that he should not be found out?

Edward. I suppose not, mother; for I have heard that he has stolen a knife since he has been in prison, and that he was confined to his cell three days for doing it, and had nothing but bread and water.

Mother. Then his sorrow is worth nothing. He is a thief still. *He is sorry only because he is punished.* He has no regard for the good of others. He has no regard for the laws. He would break them again, if he could do it and not be detected.

William. I suppose, mother, that the kind of sorrow which this man has, is nothing like true repentance.

Mother. I was just going to say the same thing, my son; and I am glad to see that you have thought of it yourself, without my telling you.

No; true repentance is a very different kind of sorrow for sin.

If *the only sorrow* which you feel for having done what God forbids you to do, or for not having done what he commands you to do, is because you fear the punishment which he has threatened against those who break his laws, then you have no true repentance for your sins.

Such sorrow does not, in itself, show that you feel

that you have done wrong. It does not show that
you have any love to God, or that you wish to honor
him by obeying his commands. It does not show
that you are willing, cheerfully, and from the heart,
to submit to his authority. It does not show that you
have any desire to do good to others; for if you had
such a desire, you would love to obey the laws of
God which he has given his creatures to make them
good and happy.

CHAPTER VII.

Further illustrations of the same topic. Not wrong to wish
to escape future punishment. Case of the poor boy's selfish sorrow.

Mother. We saw last evening, my children, that
there may be one kind of sorrow felt for our having
sinned, and yet no true repentance in the heart.

I wish, with regard to this kind of sorrow, to ask
William some questions.

William. What are they, mother?

Mother. You have at different times felt sorry that
you have disobeyed me.

William. Yes, mother.

Mother. Now, tell me why you felt sorry.

William. I think it was because I knew I had done wrong, and feared you would be displeased with me, and perhaps punish me.

Mother. Well, you saw, as you had feared, that I was displeased with you; or, in some cases, you suffered the punishment which I had threatened against disobedience.

After my displeasure, or the punishment, was over, how did you feel then?

William. I felt relieved. Sometimes I very soon forgot all about the disobedience, and the displeasure or punishment. Sometimes I thought of them a little longer, and that I would never do so again.

Mother. Why did you think that you would never do so again?

William. Because I knew I should have to suffer your displeasure or the punishment again.

Mother. In all this, have you thought that, in disobeying me, you have shown that you had no proper regard to my *rightful authority as the head of the family*, and to those rules or laws which are necessary for the good order and happiness of the whole family; and has this made you feel sorry that you have disobeyed me?

William. I am afraid, mother, that I have not thought and felt so.

Mother. Have you thought, when you disobeyed

me, that your disobedience was wrong and wicked, even if I had threatened no punishment against it; and has this made you feel sorry that you have disobeyed me?

William. I cannot say, mother, that I have thought and felt so.

Mother. Well, once more, my son. Sometimes you have disobeyed me, and were fearing the punishment I had threatened, but it so happened that your disobedience was not known to any one except yourself and your God. Time enough passed away to lead you to believe that you would never be found out. Did you feel sorry then, that you had been wicked and disobeyed me?

William. I felt a little displeased with myself; but I must say that I did not feel *as sorry for having done wrong*, as I did when I thought I should be found out, and that you would punish me.

Mother. And sometimes you have not felt sorry at all, but done the same thing again, for the very reason that you had not been found out, and that you hoped still to escape detection.

William. That is true, mother.

Mother. What William has said of himself I have no doubt is true of you too, Eliza and Edward. You have felt sorry at different times for having disobeyed me, because you feared my displeasure, or the punishment which I had threatened. And this has been the principal, if not the only reason why you have felt sorry.

Now, you know that you can have *this kind of sorrow*, and yet continue *to like to disobey me*, when what I command interferes with your own pleasure or convenience. You can have this kind of sorrow, and yet like to do the same thing again, especially if you think that I shall not know it.

This kind of sorrow, as you see, is very different from true repentance.

William. But, mother, is it wrong to fear the displeasure of God, and the punishment which he has threatened against sin?

Eliza. I was thinking about that too, mother.

Mother. It is not wrong, my children. If it were wrong to have this fear, God would not have said so much to us in the Bible about escaping from the punishment which he has threatened against sin.

He warns you to escape from it, because it will make you—*you*, William, *you*, Eliza, *you*, Edward, unhappy and wretched for ever.

He urges you, too, to cease from sin; to repent of it; to trust in Christ, " who is exalted a prince and a Savior, to give repentance and remission of sins;" and to imitate his example in doing the will of God, that you may go to heaven, and be happy there for ever.

He certainly would not do this, if it were wrong for you to think of yourself, of your own deliverance from suffering, and of your own particular good, when you feel sorry for your sins and repent of them.

But what I have been endeavoring to teach you, is, that *a great deal more than this* is necessary.

If the fear of punishment is *the only reason* why you are sorry that you have sinned, then you have not truly repented of your sins. There must be other and *stronger* reasons.

Suppose William should find a poor little boy in the street, hungry and cold, without any parents or friend to take care of him. Suppose I should tell William that he might bring this orphan into our house, and take care of him, and be a father to him. Suppose William should take some of the money which his uncle gave him, and buy clothes for the little boy, and books, and all that was necessary for his comfort and improvement.

Well, the little boy is very happy, and glad to live with us; and William, too, takes a great deal of pleasure in having Robert (for we will suppose that to be his name) behave well, and do as he is told to do

I tell William that he may see if he can govern Robert, and, in this respect also, be a father to him.

William is pleased with the plan, and sets about it with a good deal of resolution. Things go on quite well for some time; but there happens to be one affair which causes trouble.

William has promised Eliza, and Edward, and Robert, that he will show them all, the book of beautiful pictures which his aunt gave him, the next Saturday afternoon. They will have the most leisure to see it then, and his mother has told **him** it is best to put it off till that time.

In the meanwhile, as William knows that Robert has a very great curiosity to look at pictures, and has often injured them, and that he has disobeyed him in taking books when he was forbidden to do it, he tells Robert he must not take the new picture-book from the shelf, and that, if he does, he shall have nothing but bread and water for two meals.

In the afternoon, Robert is alone in the room where the picture-book is. He thinks what a pleasant time he can have in looking at the pictures. He wishes greatly to see them. He thinks, also, of the bread and water for two meals. He does not like that; for he heard that there was to be a pudding at dinner, of which he is very fond.

He thinks, too, that he shall do wrong in taking the book. He knows he has injured pictures before, and that he may injure this book, which he heard William say cost a good deal of money.

He thinks how kind William has been to him,

and that *it is right*, that he should obey him. He cannot help thinking of this. His conscience tells him that it was perfectly right for William to forbid his taking the book, and that it will *be better for him and the other children* to look at it together, when William also can explain the pictures to them.

But his curiosity is very great. His desire to see the book increases. He disregards what his conscience says he ought to do—to obey William. He takes the book and sits down by the fire to examine the pictures.

It is a large book, and he is not very careful in holding it. It falls from his hand into the fire; and before he can take it out, it has got considerably burned, and many of the pictures are spoiled. Most of them are more or less injured.

At this moment William comes in. Robert is all in confusion and alarm. He confesses what he has done, and with tears in his eyes tells William how sorry, how *very sorry* he is that it has happened.

Now suppose, my children, that Robert feels sorry only because he sees that William is displeased with him, and that he must have bread and water for two meals, and lose the pudding.

His punishment is the only thing that he fears, and is thinking about. This is the only reason why he feels sorry.

He is not sorry because he has done wrong in disobeying a good and just command of William, who had a right to make it, and who has been, too, so very kind to him.

He is not sorry at the unhappiness which William must feel in having such a valuable book injured.

He is not sorry at the disappointment which all the children must feel, and at the loss of their pleasure in not looking at the beautiful pictures.

He is not sorry for thus showing both himself and others that he has a disobedient temper, which is wrong in itself, which he has indulged before, and which there is reason to fear he will indulge again.

He is not sorry that he has set a bad example to the other children, and that they may be led by it to do wrong, and disobey the commands of their mother and teacher. He is sorry only because he will have nothing but bread and water for two meals, and lose the pudding.

Now, William, what would you think of *such kind of sorrow* for such an act of disobedience, and for the injury done to such a valuable book?

William. I must say, mother, I should feel that such a boy, for whom I had done so much, was both a very wicked boy, and very ungrateful to me for all my kindness to him.

Edward. I would make him eat bread and water a whole week.

Eliza. I would not do any such thing. I would turn him out of the house immediately, and have nothing more to do with him.

Mother. Edward and Eliza, you do not show a right temper in what you have just said.

The boy, in the case which I have supposed, acted very wrong. He might, however, have done something much worse. It was not merely his taking the book, or his carelessness, and the great injury which was done, to which I wished to direct your attention.

I wished to have you notice *the kind of sorrow* which he felt, that you might see how *entirely selfish* it was, and that it showed *no change for the better in his feelings;* nothing that would lead him *to do better* in future, if, while doing wrong, he could only be sure of avoiding detection.

You have all expressed a strong disapprobation of such *selfish sorrow.* It is right that you should disapprove of it; though Edward and Eliza would, I fear, have treated the little boy too severely, if he had been under their care.

Now think, my children, how all this shows, that *your sorrow is selfish,* if, in feeling sorry for your sins, you regard *only the punishment* which God has threatened against sin. Such a sorrow does not show that there is any change in you for the better. If God had not threatened any punishment against sin, or if it were possible for you to believe that he would never find out your sin, such a sorrow would not lead you to avoid sinning in future.

But our conversation has been rather longer than usual. We will take up the subject again to-morrow evening.

CHAPTER VIII.

Confession of sin may be made, and its guilt felt, without true repentance. True repentance something more than a strong resolution to leave off sinning, and to love and obey God.

Mother. The boy, William, who you suspected stole your ball last week, came here this afternoon and brought it back.

William. Did he acknowledge that he had stolen it, mother?

Mother. Yes; he did. He said that he felt very sorry for having stolen it, and hoped that I would forgive him, and not tell any body of it.

Edward. Well, that boy, mother, I should think really repented of what he had done.

Mother. I will not say positively that he did not, and yet I have many doubts with regard to it.

William. Why, mother?

Mother. Because *the confessing of sin does not always show that the person who makes the confession truly repents of it.*

I have heard of this boy's confessing his guilt in the same way before. When he discovers, from the conduct of others towards him, that he is suspected, and that there is a considerable probability of his being found out, he begins to think what it will be best for him to do.

Sometimes, as I know, he concludes to deny the whole matter, and see if his lying will not clear him.

At other times he fears this will not answer, and that his falsehood will surely be found out, and concludes to confess his guilt, as the only way left of escaping punishment.

Now, if he thought and felt so when he came here this afternoon, and confessed that he had stolen the ball, you all see that there was no true repentance in it.

There was *no change in him for the better*, nothing that would lead him to avoid stealing in future, if he thought that he could do it without being detected.

Eliza. But, mother, you have taught us that it is

our duty never to deny that we have done wrong, but to confess it to you at once.

Mother. So I have, my daughter; and it is right that you should do so. It was right for the boy to do so this afternoon.

True repentance will always lead you to make this confession of guilt to the person whom you may have disobeyed, or whom you may have wronged. And yet you may make this confession and have no true repentance, as was probably the case with the boy who came here this afternoon.

The motives, or the reasons, why the confession is made, show whether it proceeds from true repentance or not.

I cannot but think, my children, that you have often acknowledged to me that you have done wrong because you feared that I should certainly find it out, and you might as well have the credit of confessing it. You have thought, too, that to confess it would make the punishment lighter, or perhaps free you from all punishment.

And sometimes, when you had scarcely any fear of being detected, *your conscience made you feel uneasy.* You knew that you had done wrong, and you felt unhappy. You thought that you should feel less unhappy in confessing your guilt. You almost thought that your guilt would be done away by confessing it, and that I should think nearly as well of you as if you had not done wrong at all.

Now, if these were the only reasons why you confessed to me, at any time, that you had done wrong, it did not proceed from any true repentance; and you know that it did not.

William. I see, mother, that you understand a great deal about our feelings; and I see, too, that true repentance is a very serious matter.

Mother. Indeed it is, my son; and I wish to have you all feel that it is so.

What I have been telling you this evening, is to show you that *you may confess your sins to God, and in doing it, feel that you are guilty in his sight,* and yet have no true repentance in your hearts.

You may do all this entirely from the fear of that punishment which God threatens against sin. You may hope that in some way or other your confession may cause God to be less displeased with you, and that he will punish you less severely, or perhaps not at all.

A confession of sin to God, from no other motives than these, does not show that there is *any change for the better in your feelings towards him*, or that you will love him any more, or obey him any better in future.

He looks into your hearts. He knows all your inmost thoughts and feelings. You can hide nothing from him. If you confess your sins to him, he knows *why* you make this confession. You cannot deceive him as you may sometimes have deceived me. " There is no darkness where the workers of iniquity can hide themselves." " God searches the heart."

Remember these things, my dear children, and that the confession of sin to God, however full it may be, if made merely from the fear of punishment, is no part of true repentance.

It must be made from other and higher motives, as we shall see hereafter.

William. Are there any other *false kinds of repentance*, mother ?

Mother. Before I answer that question, William, let me ask *you* one. You recollect how sick you were last summer, and that we all thought you would die. You thought so yourself.

Do you recollect how sorry you told me you felt that you had sinned against God ?

William. I do, mother, and also how I promised God in my prayers, that if he would spare my life, I would leave off sinning, and love and obey him.

Mother. Did you think at the time that you were repenting of sin ?

William. I did, mother.

Mother. What made you think so?

William. It seemed as if it must be so; I made such *a strong resolution* to love and obey God in future.

Mother. What do you think now of that resolution, my son?

William. Ah! mother, how often I have broken it! I am afraid I made it only because I was so fearful that I should die.

Mother. If that was *the only reason* why you made it, it did not show that you felt any true repentance for your sins.

True repentance is something more than a mere strong resolution or purpose that you will leave off sinning, and begin to love and obey God.

Such a resolution may be made without any clear and affecting views of what sin is. The person who makes it may not feel what a guilty sinner he is in the sight of God. He may not see and feel that the law which condemns him is holy, just, and good. He may not feel *the evil of his own sins,* as committed against a Being who has a right to his perfect love and obedience, and who has been so full of kindness and of long-suffering towards him. He may not feel that his wicked heart is enmity against God. He may not feel the need—guilty, undone, and wretched as he is—of casting himself upon the mere mercy of God, through Jesus Christ, and of relying solely on this Savior for the pardon of his sins, and for acceptance with God.

Some other feelings, some other motives, may have led him to form the resolution which he regards as *his beginning of love and obedience to God.*

But whatever these feelings and motives may be, if those which I have just been describing are entirely wanting, the resolution, or purpose, however strong, is no part of true repentance.

There is great danger of persons being deceived in this matter.

You have reason, William, to fear that you were deceived with regard to the resolution that you formed while you were sick.

And in health, too, there is great need of careful self-examination, to see if all is right in the heart. For the Bible assures us, that "the heart is deceitful above all things, and desperately wicked."

I wish now, Edward, to ask you a question.

Sometimes, when you have done wrong, and feared my displeasure, have you not thought, *very strongly*, that you would never do so again?

Edward. O yes, mother, many times.

Mother. How did you feel after this thinking strongly, or resolution?

Edward. I felt a great deal better. For it seemed

to me as if I should, all at once, be a good boy, and not do wrong any more.

Mother. Did you not feel as if you had done something very good in making such a resolution?

Edward. How did you know that I felt so, mother? For I never told you that I did.

Mother. Did you at the same time feel truly sorry that you had done wrong?

Edward. At first, mother, I felt sorry, for I feared you would know it. But after I had made what you call the resolution, I think I did not feel quite so sorry.

Mother. Well, Edward, how have you kept your resolutions?

Edward. I am obliged to say, mother, that I have not kept them very well.

Mother. Ah! my son, I hope you, and the other children, will never forget what I am about to say to you, as we close the conversation of this evening.

Resolutions to leave off sinning, and to love and obey God, will be of no use to you, unless they proceed from a heartfelt repentance for your sins, as committed against a wise, holy, just, and good God.

Such resolutions will be of no use to you, unless you feel, also, a sincere reliance on Jesus Christ as your only Savior, and trust in him, as a poor, guilty, condemned sinner, for forgiveness and acceptance with God.

Such resolutions will be of no use to you, if they are made in your own strength. You must beseech God, for Christ's sake, to give you the Holy Spirit, that you may be renewed and strengthened to keep them. Thus *be strong in the Lord, and in the power of his might,* and there will be hope that your good resolutions will not be like *the morning cloud, and the early dew, which appear for a little time, and then vanish away.*

CHAPTER IX.

Repentance for one sin, if sincere, will be accompanied with repentance for all sins. Self-reproach. Case of Judas.

Mother. It is a month, Edward, since I had to reprove you for taking down the large book of plates in the library. I believe you have not meddled with it again.

Edward. I have not, mother.

Eliza. But he has been to work, to-day, at the drawer of shells.

Mother. You knew what pains I had taken, my son, to put them in order. I hope you have not disturbed them.

Eliza. Indeed he has, mother. He had them out,

playing with them. It will take you a long time to put them in order again.

Mother. How could you do so, Edward, after having told me how *very sorry* you felt that you had disobeyed me in taking down the book of plates?

Edward. Mother, you did not forbid me to take the shells.

Mother. That is true. But, in forbidding you to meddle with the book of plates, I gave you reasons which you could not help understanding as applying to the drawer of shells also. I told you that I wished, particularly, to keep every thing in the library in perfect order; and that your great curiosity to meddle with every thing, I feared, would trouble me.

Edward. I am *very sorry*, mother, that I took out the shells; indeed I am.

Mother. And will your sorrow for this keep you from meddling with every thing else in the library?

Edward. I hope it will, mother.

Mother. Well, we will see, my son. But learn, from your conduct, that you may give up doing wrong *in one particular way*, and yet have no true repentance.

If you had had *the right kind of sorrow* for disobeying me in taking down the book of plates, you would not have meddled with the drawer of shells.

Just so, my children, you may cease to commit some particular sin against God, and think that you have truly repented of it. But how can this be, if you go on sinning in other respects?

Because a child no longer disobeys his father or mother in one thing, yet continues to be disobedient in many other things, you all see that is no proof whatever of his having truly repented of his wrong conduct in that one thing.

Besides, as you grow older, your fondness for different objects will change. Edward would find it exceedingly difficult now to give up his marbles. If I should, for any reason, forbid his playing with them, he would think it a very hard command, and, I fear he would be very strongly tempted to break it.

But if we should both live till he gets to be eighteen years old, and I should forbid him to play with marbles, there would be no danger at all of his disobedience.

There would be other things, however, which young men of that age are as fond of as Edward is now of his marbles, and to give up which, at the command of his mother, would be a hard matter, and he might be tempted to disobey me.

You must take great care, therefore, my children, lest, in simply *losing a fondness* for something which once led you to do wrong, you think that you have truly repented of your wrong conduct, because you find that you can give the thing up readily and cheerfully.

Many persons, as they grow older, or from a change in their situation, deceive themselves greatly in this respect.

Grown-up persons often change the objects of which they are fond, as much as children do.

A man who is confined to his room by sickness, and knows that he cannot go abroad, may think that he has quite given up his former desire to ride out for amusement on the Sabbath. He may even think that he feels truly sorry that he ever did it.

But let his health be restored. That will show whether his sorrow is true repentance for sin. Besides, how can he dare to think it is so, while he breaks the Sabbath as much as he ever did, by reading books, in his sick room, which are not suited to the day?

Never forget, my children, that *repentance for one sin, if sincere, will be accompanied with repentance for all sins;* and that forsaking one sin is no proof of its being truly repented of, unless there is a constant effort and prayer to forsake all sins, and to do all that God requires of you.

What I have been describing is a kind of false

repentance, of which there is a great deal, both among grown persons and children, and which, I hope, you will not fail to remember.

William. Sometimes, mother, after I have done wrong, I feel very much displeased with myself. I think what a foolish and wicked boy I have been. It makes me feel bad to think ill of myself, just as it does to have you think ill of me.

Mother. That shows, my son, what conscience is. Such feelings are called *self-reproach.* Your conscience leads you to see and to feel your guilt, and you reproach yourself for it in the same way as if another person, acquainted with your guilt, should do it.

William. Is that true repentance?

Mother. It is always found where there is true repentance. But it *may be felt* where there is nothing like true repentance.

Those who are not hardened in sin, feel this self-reproach deeply, when they do what their consciences tell them they ought not to do.

It ought to lead them to true repentance. For it shows what a dreadful evil sin is, which can thus, *itself, make the sinner wretched,* by being his own tormenter. It shows how those who die without repentance, and are sent into the world of despair, will inflict upon themselves the most severe part of their sufferings.

It shows how holy, just, and good the law of God is, which condemns the sinner. For this law is made because *there is a real and great difference between right and wrong.* And the sinner's own conscience perceives, and feels this difference between what is right and what is wrong.

It shows how earnestly the sinner ought to desire to be freed from sin, that he may be restored to the favor and friendship of God. For if *he* sees enough in his guilt to lead him thus to reproach himself, and to feel ashamed and degraded in his own opinion, *what must God think of him?* How must he appear in the sight of a Being who is perfectly pure and holy, and who cannot look on sin but with the utmost abhorrence?

And yet this self-reproach, very bitter and painful as it is, may exist, and there be no true repentance in the heart.

Judas, the wicked and ungrateful disciple who betrayed Christ, must have felt this self-reproach in a very high degree.

His conduct shows that he did. When he saw in what his base betraying of his Lord and Master had ended, and that Christ was condemned to death, *he repented himself.*

He felt how very wickedly he had acted; he was *sorry* for it, and wished that he had not betrayed Christ.

It was not the right kind of repentance, however. For, if I had time, I could easily show you that there are two kinds of repentance spoken of in the Bible. One is such as Judas had, without any *change for the better in his feelings*—a sorrow for sin only because he felt its shame and reproach, and dreaded the just displeasure of God against it; but without any real hatred of sin, as wrong in itself, and without any love to God, and obedience to his commands.

The other kind of repentance, spoken of in the Bible, is what I expect yet to explain to you.

"Judas brought again the thirty pieces of silver to the chief priests and elders, saying, I have sinned in that I have betrayed the innocent blood. And they said, What is that to us? See thou to that. And he cast down the pieces of silver in the temple, and departed, and went and hanged himself."

What a striking instance of self-reproach on account of sin!

And yet there was no true repentance connected with it. Had there been, Judas would have shown a far different spirit from what he did. He would not have rushed madly upon the violation of one of the positive commands of God, by taking his own life. He would have desired to live, that he might humble himself before God and his fellow-men; and that he might, if possible, in some way, repair the wrong which he had done to Christ, and to his cause.

There is great danger, my children, of your mistaking the self-reproach of which we have been speaking, for true repentance. It is a painful feeling, and you suffer under it. You may think that you are the better for such suffering. You may almost imagine that it is a kind of punishment for sin, which, being endured, the sin is done away, and will be forgiven.

But forget not that this self-reproach, in itself alone, is not true repentance. Other views and feelings are necessary. Be not deceived in this respect; and let the example of Judas, who gave such a striking illustration of this self-reproach without any true repentance, be fixed in your memory.

CHAPTER X.

Reparation may be made, and forgiveness implored, without true repentance. Recapitulation.

Mother. You will think, my children, that this subject in which we are engaged, is a long one; but I hope you will not find it tedious. Perhaps I may not again have the opportunity of explaining it fully to you. For life is uncertain; and I feel that if I have any one duty which I ought most faithfully to perform, it is to show you *how you may secure the eternal friendship of Jesus, the Savior.* And there is but one way in which you can do this, *by going to him, a repenting and believing sinner.*

How important, then, that you should understand what true repentance is, and that I should endeavor fully to explain it to you!

Eliza, Edward tells me that you have given him one of your prettiest books, to pay him for breaking his little wagon yesterday, in such a bad temper.

Eliza. I was sorry that I got angry with him, and broke the wagon. He is very welcome to the book. And I asked him to forgive me. Did he tell you that too, mother?

Mother. Yes, he did. But remember, my daughter, it is one thing to make reparation for a wrong, and to ask forgiveness ; it is quite another, to feel truly sorry that you have done the wrong, and to feel this sorrow from right motives.

Eliza. If I do right, mother, why need I trouble myself so much to find out what the motives are ?

Mother. Because *you cannot do right, if your motives are wrong.*

If you felt sorry for the wrong which you did in breaking your brother's wagon in anger, *only* because you feared that I should inflict some punishment upon you, your motive was altogether selfish. Such sorrow did not show that there was *any change in you for the better*, or that you would not be likely to get angry again and do wrong, if you thought you could do so and escape my notice of it.

In the same way, if you gave him the book, and asked his forgiveness, *only* that you might feel as if you had *paid him off* for breaking his wagon, your motive was altogether selfish. You might think that in this way you could get rid of the reproaches of conscience, and that your wrong conduct might all be forgotten, and trouble you no longer, since you had *given up so much*, and done him, indeed, a greater benefit than you had done him injury.

In addition to all this, you might think that your making reparation, and asking forgiveness, would lead me to praise you, and call you a good girl, and forget entirely all that had happened. And so you would escape *my reproof and advice about doing better in future*, as well as the reproaches of your own conscience.

If those were the motives, my daughter, which led you to give your brother the book and to ask his forgiveness, there was nothing in your thoughts and feelings of true repentance.

The same kind of selfish motives may lead you, my children, to make reparation for wrong conduct in other instances, and even to ask forgiveness of God, without having the least true repentance for your sins.

You may think that, by making such reparation, or by doing some good thing in the way of charity to others, or by obeying, in your outward conduct, some command of God, you may render him less displeased with you, and less likely to punish you.

You may think that, in this way, you can even go so far as *to pay God* for the dishonor which you have shown him, and by giving up something that you value very much, or by doing something that costs you much time and effort, do him a greater benefit than you have done him injury.

You may think that, in this way, you can feel at ease in your conscience, and give yourself no further trouble about your sinful conduct.

This is not the repentance which God requires. Some persons have called it repentance. They have gone even so far as to think that by doing something which is very difficult and tiresome, or by inflicting pain and suffering upon themselves, they could make *reparation to God* for their disobedience of his laws. They have thought that they could in this way obtain his favor, *by deserving it.*

As you grow older, my children, you may be more likely than you now are to have such thoughts and feelings as I have been describing. You will be in great danger of mistaking them for true repentance. Indeed, you have some such thoughts and feelings now under my government, and with regard to your conduct in the family. Eliza, I fear, has shown this in the motives which led her to make reparation to her brother and to ask his forgiveness.

Look at the motives, my children, which lead you to make reparation, and to ask forgiveness, either of your fellow-men or of God.

These motives, if they are right, will proceed from love. You will feel love to God, and love to others. You will love to obey God, because he is so wise, and just, and holy, and good. You will love to do good to others, that you may be like God, who desires to make his creatures happy.

If you have sinned against God, in breaking any

of his laws, or in doing any injury to others, the love of which I have spoken will lead you to repent of it, and to show that you do thus repent of it, by asking forgiveness of God, and of your fellow-men, and by making all the reparation in your power. And this shows you the necessity of having your heart renewed by the Holy Spirit.

Without this feeling of love to God, and to men, all that you may do in the way of making reparation for sin is no part of true repentance. *Good works*, as they are called, of whatever kind, if they do not proceed from such love, are no proof of true repentance.

Hear what the Apostle Paul says on this subject, in the thirteenth chapter of his first Epistle to the Corinthians:

" *Though I bestow all my goods to feed the poor, and though I give my body to be burned, and have not charity,* (or love to God and to men,) *it profiteth me nothing.*" And your heart must be renewed by the Holy Spirit, that you may have this love.

William. Mother, when will you tell us what true repentance is?

Mother. I am nearly ready to do that, and I hope to do it so much the better from having explained to you, at some length, what is *not* repentance, or what may be thought and felt *without truly repenting of sin.*

Before we conclude our conversation this evening, I will go over again, very briefly, what I have been explaining to you for some evenings past. It will help to fix it in your memory, and to prepare you the better to understand what I am yet to teach you.

If *the only sorrow* which you feel for having done what God forbids you to do, or for not having done what he commands you to do, is because you fear *the punishment* which he has threatened against those who break his laws, then you have no true repentance for your sins.

If God had *not threatened* any punishment against sin, or if it were possible for you to believe that he would *not find out* your sin, and you should still continue to love to sin, this would show that you had not truly repented of your sins.

You may *confess* your sins to God, and in doing it, feel that you are guilty in his sight, and yet have no true repentance in your hearts. You may do this entirely from the fear of punishment. You may hope that your confession may cause God to be less displeased with you, and that he will punish you less severely, or perhaps not at all. If these are your only motives in confessing your sins to God, it does not show that you truly repent of them.

True repentance is something more than a mere *strong resolution* or purpose that you will leave off

sinning, and begin to love and obey God. Such a resolution will be of no use unless it proceeds from a
heart-felt sorrow for your sins, as committed against
a wise, holy, just and good God. It will be of no
use, unless you feel also *a sincere reliance on Jesus
Christ* as your only Savior. It will be of no use, if it
is made in your own strength. In making it, you
must beseech God, for Christ's sake, to give you the
Holy Spirit, that you may be strengthened to keep
it, and be renewed in the temper of your mind.

You may *cease to commit some particular sin*
against God, and think that you have truly repented
of it. This cannot be, if you go on sinning in other
respects. It would be only getting tired of one sin,
and changing it for others. Repentance for one sin,
if sincere, will be accompanied with repentance for
all sins. Forsaking one sin is no proof of its being
truly repented of, unless there is a constant effort and
prayer to forsake all sins, and to do all that God requires of you.

You may feel great and painful *self-reproach* for
sin, as Judas did, and yet not truly repent of it. You
may ask *forgiveness* of God, and of your fellow-men,
and make *reparation* for injuries done to others, and
in this way, and by your *good works*, hope to ease
your conscience and obtain the favor of God, with
out truly repenting of your sins.

CHAPTER XI.

True repentance leads to new views of God, and of his right to our entire love and obedience; to deep sorrow for ingratitude towards God; to new views of the laws of God, and of guilt in having broken them.

Mother. Now, my children, we are prepared to attend more particularly to the consideration of what true repentance is.

In doing this, I wish you to recollect that all persons who truly repent of sin, do not have precisely the same thoughts and feelings *in the same order.*

I shall describe to you many thoughts and feelings which those have who truly repent of their sins. They will not have *all of them* when they first feel this repentance. But if they live, they will have them sooner or later, and more and more strongly.

Some persons may have some of these thoughts and feelings much sooner than other persons have them, and not in the order in which I shall mention them. Some persons may have some of these thoughts and feelings much more clearly and strongly than others have them.

Some persons, also, in repenting of their sins, have *much more dread of future punishment* than others have. This desire of deliverance from the awful displeasure of God, and from the misery, in the future world, of those who die impenitent, may be very strong in some who truly repent of their sins. It does not show that their repentance is not sincere. It often accompanies true repentance, and is mingled with other thoughts and feelings, which I shall presently begin to describe.

Some who have little or nothing of this fear of future punishment, are much affected when they are led to repent of their sins, by *the desire of future happiness in heaven.* They have found out that this world cannot make them happy. They have heard the kind and gracious invitations of God to come unto him with repentance for sin, and faith in the Lord Jesus Christ, and his encouraging promises, that all who do come in this way shall be accepted of him, and made perfectly happy in his presence for ever.

This desire of future happiness by no means shows that their repentance is insincere. It always, in a greater or less degree, accompanies true repentance, and is mingled with the other thoughts and feelings which constitute it. But the avoidance of future misery, or the obtaining of future happiness, are not the only objects to which the attention and feelings of the true penitent are directed. Other and greater objects than *his own personal good*, call forth his most fixed attention, and wake up his most powerful feelings.

He looks up to God, and thinks of him as he never did before. He thinks of him as the being by whom he was made, who has continued to keep him in life, and who has given him every thing that he has, and that he enjoys.

He thinks of God as having, therefore, *a right* to his entire love and obedience.

He feels that he has *done wrong* in not rendering to God this love and obedience. He feels that he has no excuse to make for not doing it. He feels that his own sinfulness and self-will have led him to refuse to do it. He acknowledges the great guilt of his pride and obstinacy of heart. He is truly and deeply sorry for it. His will, subdued and humbled, bows in submission to the will of God; not as if forced to do it, as when a child yields to the will of the parent from the fear of punishment, but he freely, fully and cheerfully desires and endeavors to do it, and trusts to Christ to aid him in doing it.

His will bows in submission to the will of God, *in all things*. He is willing that God should do with him as seemeth best in his sight, in leading him to holiness and to heaven.

He thinks of God as having been *exceedingly*

kind to him. He looks back upon his past life and sees how many comforts, and mercies, and privileges he has received from his heavenly Father.

How many others have had few, or scarcely any of these blessings! He has not deserved to be treated differently from them. Indeed, he wonders that he has not been treated worse than they. For many of them have not known their duty as well as he has known his.

God has shown great forbearance and long suffering towards him in not depriving him of all his blessings, of which he has made so poor a use, and in not cutting him down in the midst of his sins.

And, above all this, what great and wonderful love God has shown towards him and his fellow-sinners, in sending his only and well-beloved Son into the world to die on the cross, that all who trust in him might be pardoned and saved!

He has heard of this Savior, this kind and compassionate Savior; this friend and hope of sinners; this deliverer from death and hell; this all-sufficient and Almighty Redeemer. He has been invited, and urged, and warned, again and again, to go to him; to believe on him; to be saved by him; and to be happy now and for ever.

He has sinned against all this goodness of God;

he has sinned against all this compassion of Christ. He sees his guilt as he never saw it before.

He feels that he has been *a most perverse and ungrateful sinner.* He mourns over his ingratitude. He confesses it to God. He feels like a little child desirous of returning, humble and broken-hearted, to the kind father whom he has offended. He returns, too, *in the way* which his heavenly Father has pointed out.

He knows that God will not receive him unless he comes *believing on the Lord Jesus Christ,* and trusting entirely to what *he* has done and suffered for acceptance with God.

He does thus rely on this Savior, and full of guilt as he is, believes the promises of God through Christ; and casting himself upon his mercy, he feels that now, if ever, his sorrow for his sins should be the deepest. For it was *his sins* that made it necessary that the Savior should suffer and die. And his guilt appears to him great indeed; *his ingratitude of the vilest kind,* when he considers how long he has continued to reject this Savior, and to slight this mercy of God. Here, truly, he finds cause for repentance, for tears, for groans, for deep anguish of soul!

The true penitent looks up to God, and thinks of *his laws* as he never did before.

He sees that, like God himself, they are holy, just,

and good; that it is right and best that God should make such laws, and be honored and obeyed by all the beings whom he has formed.

He sees that God was very good in making these laws, and that, if all *would obey them*, all would form *one great family of love*, happy in loving and serving God, and in loving others, and seeing them good and happy.

He feels that he has been very selfish and wicked in not obeying these laws.

Once he thought them severe, and perpetually interfering with his own comfort and enjoyment.

He now feels that they are just what are necessary to promote his own happiness in connexion with the happiness of others, and to guide him in the way of duty and of peace. He feels that he is justly condemned for having broken these laws, and that his only hope of escaping their penalty is by trusting in Christ.

He mourns over his past disobedience to God, and the earnest desire of his soul is, that in future he may understand all that God requires of him, and perform it with a willing and obedient heart.

To-morrow evening, my children, we will see, still further, what true repentance is.

CHAPTER XII.

The penitent has new views of sin, as committed against
God. He has a strong hatred of sin. He confesses his
sins to God. He mourns over his guilt, in not having
sought to do good to others.

William. What you explained to us last evening,
mother, shows that a very great change must take
place in the thoughts and feelings of a person who
truly repents of sin.

Mother. That is true, my son; but I have more yet
to tell you of this change, from which you will see
that it is indeed a great and surprising one.

*The true penitent thinks of sin as he never did
before.*

Formerly, it appeared to him a small evil. He
thought of it lightly. He, perhaps, spoke of it lightly;
or, as wicked persons are apt to do, he might even
laugh about it.

If he was ever led to think of it seriously at all, it
was not as an offence against a holy and just God,
but as what might expose him to the punishment
threatened against sin.

Its consequences to himself was all that he was
looking at.

Now he regards sin in a very different light. He
sees that it is a very great evil, and principally so, *as*

committed against God. *All his sins* appear to him to have been committed against God. For they were all violations of the two great laws of love to God and to his fellow-men, which God has given us, and which we are bound at all times to obey.

He feels that his guilt in having done wrong to others, or in not having sought to do them good, although very great, is small, compared with his guilt in having sinned against God.

He sees what dreadful evils would take place if all were to sin against God as he has done, and continue to do so; how God would be dishonored; and disorder, and confusion, and misery prevail among all beings.

He feels that, so far as he has sinned, he has shown a disposition to produce these evils—to oppose the government of God, and to make others wretched.

This fills him with the deepest sorrow. He mourns over his sins as offences against God. He laments the injury which his sins have done to others. He is exceedingly pained at the thought of having encouraged others to sin by his influence or example, and of having been the means, perhaps, of helping them on in the way to everlasting destruction.

All this is accompanied with his very strong *hatred of sin.*

Were there no punishment threatened against sin, still he would hate it as the worst of evils.

He loathes his own past sinful feelings and con- duct. He cannot think of them without shame and self-reproach. He feels how sin has debased him ; how useless, and worse than useless, he has been among the creatures of God; how unworthy of the esteem of virtuous and holy beings; how deserving of being sent to dwell for ever with those who are as degraded and as unworthy as himself.

He hates sin also in others. He desires to have them freed from it. He longs to have the time come when all shall hate it as he does, and when he and they shall overcome it, and the will of God be done on earth as it is done in heaven.

The true penitent does not wish *to cover up his sins.* He is willing to know how guilty he is.

Formerly he was very reluctant to have any one tell him even his faults. Now he is ready to hear not only what his smaller offences against God and his fellow-men have been, but the greater ones also. He receives admonition and reproof with meek- ness. He desires to see and to feel in what respects he has erred or sinned, and prays to God to enable him to do this.

He confesses his sins to God. He does this with- out keeping any back. He does it with a broken and contrite heart. He does it with deep humility and sorrow. He knows to what a pure and holy being he makes this confession, and he feels, in making it, how entirely he must cast himself on the mercy of God, through Christ, that he may be regarded with forgiveness and compassion.

The true penitent has new views, and very different from what he had before, with regard to the *happiness of others.*

Formely, he may have been kind and amiable in his conduct. He may have been honest and just. He may have been much beloved by his friends and acquaintances. He may have been considered by them as one who wished and endeavored to contribute to their comfort and enjoyment.

But now he sees how little he regarded their true happiness. Indeed, he finds that he did not regard it all. For he thought only of their happiness in this world, and not at all of their holiness and happiness in the next.

Besides, it was the comfort and enjoyment only of *his friends* which he almost entirely regarded, and this, too, because *his own* was so much connected with it. To give up much of any thing, or to put himself to any considerable inconvenience, that he might do good to those who were not his friends and acquaintances, did not make a part of his feelings and conduct.

He now sees *how selfish* he has been in all this; how he has forgotten God, and the Savior, and the future world, in his intercourse with his fellow-men; and how entirely he has neglected to endeavor to make them truly happy, by leading them to love and obey God.

He sees that God placed him in the world that he might do good to others, not only to their bodies, but to their souls; not only with regard to this world, but still more with regard to their eternal existence beyond the grave.

He looks to Jesus Christ. He thinks how he went about *doing good*—how, in this way, he did the will of God, and left an example for us all to follow.

He feels that he has been very neglectful of his duty in not following this example. He is deeply sorry for it.

He mourns over his past life, which has been spent in seeking his own good, and in doing little, if any thing, for the true happiness of others.

In all this he feels that he has not only failed in his duty to his fellow-men, but that he has sinned against God. For God has kept him in life, that he might spend it in doing good to others. And God has given him the ability and the means with which to do much good to others. And God has commanded him to do good to others. And his own conscience has taught him, that, by doing good to others, he would best promote his own happiness. And he has often been struck and reproved by the sight of those who were engaged in doing good to others, and has seen how much better, and nobler, and happier a course they were pursuing.

He feels the selfishness, the meanness, the guilt, *the sin against God*, of his past feelings and conduct; he desires, with his whole soul, that he may live hereafter to do good—*all the good in his power* to those around him, and to his fellow-men. He desires to do this not only to those of his own family, to his relations and friends, and acquaintances, but to all whom he can in any way benefit. He desires to do this, not only to those who are kind to him and wish to do him good, but equally so to his enemies, if he has any; to those who can never repay him for his kindness, to those who will not even thank him for it, and even to those who may return him evil for his good.

William. I think, mother, if we all felt so, we should have a very happy family.

Mother. Yes, my son, that is very true. And if all children, and all parents felt so, all families would be happy. And if all persons felt so, what happy neighborhoods we should have; what happy villages and towns, and cities; what a happy country; what a happy world!

Ah! my dear children, *you* have not felt so. Look back on your lives, short as they have been. See what has been the object of your daily conduct. What have you been seeking to obtain? When you first rose in the morning, what did you think you would do during the day, and what would you do it *for?*

And during the day, you have had some plans of doing this or that thing. You have, perhaps, got others to assist you in accomplishing these plans. Or you have formed plans for the morrow—for the next week and month—it may be, for the following years.

Your hearts have been much set upon accomplishing these plans. You expected to be very happy in accomplishing them. If you have failed, you have been greatly disappointed.

Now, in these various ways, what have you been thinking, and feeling, and conversing, and acting *for?* For *yourself,* or for *others;* for your own particular happiness, or for the happiness of others,'and your own, as connected with it?

If you will answer these questions honestly, each for yourself, you will see how much *you* need to repent of your past selfishness and sin, and to go to Christ, that by the aid of the Holy Spirit you may have love to God and the Savior—love to your fellow-men, and *an active desire to do all the good in your power.*

CHAPTER XIII.

The true penitent mourns over his guilt in having done
wrong to others. He makes reparation. He mourns over
his sins of thought and feeling, and longs to be pure in
heart. He struggles against his peculiar sins.

Mother. The latter part of our conversation, last
evening, showed you, my children, how much sorrow the true penitent feels for having done so little
to promote the real happiness of his fellow-men.

In connection with this, he thinks how much he
has done *actually to injure his fellow-men.*

He may have said or done things, in their presence, to lead them to disobey and dishonor God, to
reject the Savior, and to keep on in the ways of
sin.

He may have been dishonest in his dealings with
them, cheating them in a bargain, or, at any rate,
not doing to them as he would wish them to do to
him in similar circumstances.

He may have taken property which was not his
own, perhaps stolen it, or not returned it when he
ought to have done so.

The property of others may have been injured
by him, from design, or through his carelessness
and neglect.

He may have spoken ill of others, falsely, or more than was strictly true, or when there was no just cause for his doing it, and only to gratify his own selfish and wicked feelings.

He may have been unkind in his conduct towards others, and treated them angrily, or rudely, with pride and contempt.

He may not have acted towards his parents, and teachers, and superiors, as he ought to have done. He may have treated them with disrespect, or even insult. He may have disobeyed them, and given them a great deal of trouble.

He thinks seriously of all these ways, and of any others, too, in which he has done wrong to his fellow-men.

He sees how guilty he has been in these respects. He feels that he has sinned, not only against his fellow-men, but against God. For God has commanded him *to love his neighbor as himself; and to do to others as he would have others do to him.*

He humbles himself before God. He confesses his sin; he mourns over it. He prays that in future he may do these things no more, but regard the happiness, the property, the character, and the feelings of others as he would his own.

But he does not stop here. He inquires, he prays for direction, he consults wise and pious persons, that he may find out his duty with regard to those whom he may have injured.

Where he finds it to be his duty to confess the wrong which he has done to others, he does it promptly, frankly, fully, and humbly asks forgiveness.

He is equally careful to make reparation to the full extent of his power. If he has injured others in their property or business, he makes restitution. If he has injured them in their character, he takes pains to acknowledge to others in what way he has done it—that he has done it without cause, and that he is truly sorry for it.

He is very anxious to do away the injury which his wicked example or influence may have done to the souls of others. He seeks for opportunities of being with them, of confessing to them the error and the sinfulness of his past conduct in their society, and of intreating them to repent of *their sins*; to turn unto God; to trust in the Redeemer; and to devote themselves to his service.

I wish you, my children, to think seriously of this part of true repentance, and to see the need that you have of feeling and acting as I have just been telling you the true penitent does.

Have not each of you very often, by your example and influence, led a brother or sister, or some other child, to feel wrong, or to do wrong? Cannot you recollect many such instances?

In your little bargains, have you done to other children just as you would have them do to you? Have you never done any thing like cheating? Have you never taken the property of others without leave, and used it up, or kept it, or lost it?

Have you been careful not to injure the property of others intentionally, or by carelessness and neglect?

Have you always spoken of others as you ought to do? Cannot you recollect instances in which you have told untruths about them, or made their conduct appear worse than it really was?

Have you not often been unkind to others in your language and conduct, and sometimes given way to anger, or even to blows?

Think how often you may have looked, or spoken, or acted improperly to your parent, or teacher, or some older person, who had a right to be treated with respect and obedience; and how much pain and trouble you may, in this way, have given them.

Now all these things are sins against God. So far as you are guilty of them, you should repent of them in his presence, and beseech him, for Christ's sake, to forgive you.

But it is, also, your duty to ask those whom you have injured to forgive you, and to make them reparation for the wrongs that you have done them, so far as it is in your power.

Think of all this, my children, and learn from it what an important and serious duty true repentance is.

There is another thing which always marks the true penitent. He sees that there are *sins of thought and feeling*, as well as of conversation and conduct. Indeed, he finds out, what he little suspected before, that what *he says and does* forms but a small part of his character in the sight of God.

He sees that the laws of God reach the soul, and require that his very thoughts and feelings should be right.

He sees how many wrong thoughts and feelings he has had, how many which he would be unwilling that any person should know, and which he would be ashamed to tell to his best friend.

He remembers how many thoughts and feelings he has had which he would not dare to express in words, or act out in his conduct, and for having which, his conscience has severely reproved him.

There are other thoughts and feelings ; his pride, his vanity, his envy, his resentment, his murmuring, his discontent, and such like, which he did not think much of at the time, but which he now sees were sinful. He sees that it was by indulging such thoughts and feelings he was the more ready to *do wrong;* and that if we could have all our thoughts and feelings right, our conversation and conduct would be right also.

He sees that a being, so perfectly pure and holy as God is, must look with great abhorrence on unholy thoughts and feelings. How much then, and how often God must have looked on him with abhorrence. He is humbled and deeply sorry at the recollection of this. He feels how guilty he has been in the sight of God, even while others may have thought well of him.

His repentance goes to his inmost soul. It reaches his hidden thoughts and feelings, his purposes, his wishes, his desires, his fears, his hopes; all the secret workings and movements of his mind.

He longs to be *pure in heart.* He prays for the Holy Spirit to direct all his thoughts and feelings, and to aid and strengthen him, that he may banish every thing that is unholy from his soul; that he may have there no thoughts or feelings displeasing to God, or which he would be afraid to make known to his fellow-men.

The true penitent is sensible that there are *some sins,* both of heart and of conduct, to which he is *peculiarly liable.*

You know, my children, that it is so with you.

You know how easily Edward is led away, by his play, to neglect to do what I have told him must be done immediately, and how often I have had to reprove him on this account.

And Eliza's great fault is, the disposition to find fault with others; and William's, to command his brother and sister in an unkind way, and with too much authority, as if he were the head of the family.

Grown persons, also, have sins to which they are peculiarly liable. As you grow older you will find this to be true with regard to yourselves. You will find, if you truly repent of such sins, that it is a great work entirely to overcome them, and that you must be looking continually to God for the aids of the Holy Spirit.

The true penitent humbles himself before God on account of his peculiar sins. He confesses them all with the deepest sorrow. He wonders that he never saw them before as he does now. He prays that he may be led to discover all such sins to which he is liable, and that he may have clear and affecting views of them, as committed against God, and as injuring himself and others.

In God's strength, with faith in Christ, and with continual and devout prayer for the aids of the Holy Spirit, he begins to overcome these sins. *He begins immediately*, the very day and hour that he feels true repentance, the very moment that he has again any disposition to commit such sins. And this he does, whether they are sins of thought, of word, or of conduct.

Without this desire, and prayer, and effort to over-come such sins, there can be no true repentance.

Mark what I have just said, my children, and never forget it.

Should Edward tell me that he hoped he had truly repented of his sins, and yet show by his conduct that he was not praying and trying to obey my commands *immediately*, however pleasant and inviting his plays might be, it would be certain that he had not felt any thing like true repentance.

And if Eliza should say she had truly repented of her sins, and yet continue to show her fault-finding temper as much as ever, how sadly she would be mistaken!

And if William should hope he had truly repented of his sins, and go on indulging, just as before, his unkind, authoritative way of commanding his brother and sister, it would show, beyond all doubt, that he knew nothing, by his own feelings, of what true repentance is.

True repentance is always accompanied with earnest desires, and prayers, and efforts, to overcome the sinner's peculiar sins to which he is most liable, and shows itself in his actually overcoming them. For God will certainly strengthen the true penitent to do this by his grace.

CHAPTER XIV.

The true penitent, in the strength of God, begins the work of an entire reformation. He lives and acts to be instrumental in leading others to Christ.

Mother. In addition to what I said, my children, in our last conversation, with regard to the true penitent's overcoming his peculiar sins, I wish you to remember another thing of great importance.

He resolves, in the strength of God, to forsake all sin, and begin immediately the work of an entire reformation in his heart and life.

This is the best and surest proof of true repentance.

You have seen how great a sinner the true penitent feels himself to be, and how he humbles himself before God on that account, and sorrows for his guilt.

Up to the day and the hour of his repentance, his sins have been increasing. His thoughts, his feelings, his conversation, his conduct have been sinful. *How the power of these sins has been strengthened by habit!*

Is repentance, however strong and sincere it may be, about to do all this away in a day, in an hour, in a moment?

Ah! the true penitent soon finds that this is very far from being the case. He has a great work before him. He has a powerful enemy to overcome. He must struggle against sin as long as life lasts.

He begins the struggle immediately. He looks to God for the aids of the Holy Spirit. He seeks to enlighten his conscience by a careful perusal of the Bible and an examination of his own heart. He sets about *the work of reformation*, diligently and in earnest.

And all around him see that this reformation *has begun.* They cannot help seeing it, it is so clear and striking.

In his family, in his neighborhood, in his business, in all his intercourse with others, there is *a manifest change for the better* in his feelings, in his conversation, and in his conduct. He shows that he is indeed sorry for all that has been selfish, proud, unkind, uncharitable, unforgiving, revengeful, oppressive, unjust, ungenerous, base or mean, in his past feelings and conduct, by feeling and acting in a very different manner.

He becomes more and more benevolent, humble, and kind to all around him. He thinks as well of others as he possibly can, and is careful not to speak ill of them, unless his duty renders it absolutely necessary.

He had rather suffer wrong than do wrong. He forgives those who injure him, and tries to do them good. He wrongs no one in his dealings. In all his business he takes no advantage of others. He does to others as he would have others do to him.

At times he may fail in some of these things greatly, and at others in a less degree. When he does, he repents again and again. He struggles on. *His faith in Christ* keeps him up. *The change for the better* in all his feelings and conduct, is more and more striking every year, every month, every day.

His reformation is the proof of his repentance. Without such reformation, so far as life is spared and an opportunity given for showing it, there can be no true repentance. All else that looks like it is deceitful and false.

If either of you, my children, should tell me that you hoped you had truly repented of your sins, I should look to *the change for the better* in all your feelings and conduct—*to your reformation*, for the proof of it.

If I did not see that you were daily becoming more kind, and affectionate, and generous towards others; more desirous of making them both good and happy, and more willing to give up your own comfort and convenience to do this; if I did not see that you were daily becoming more obedient to all my commands, and more anxious to do all you could to please me, and to aid me in taking care of the family; if I did not see that you were daily becoming more benevolent to all around you, and in some good degree loving them as you did yourself, I should not believe at all that you had repented of your sins.

You might tell me ever so much about your great sorrow for your sins, and how you had confessed them to God, and prayed him to forgive you, and resolved to do as you ought to do; all this I should consider as only showing some fears of conscience, but not any true repentance.

This rule which I have given you by which to judge of true repentance, is the same that Jesus Christ gave while he was on earth.

By their fruits ye shall know them, said he.

You judge what a tree is by the fruit which it produces. If the fruit is bad, you say the tree is bad. If the fruit is good, you say the tree is good.

True repentance must bring forth good fruit in the heart, in the conversation, and in the conduct. It must do this in small things as well as in great; in all our daily intercourse with our fellow-men; in the family and in our business, as well as in our prayers and our efforts to serve God and build up the kingdom of Christ in the world.

I have still a few other things to tell you, that you may be able to judge whether repentance is true or not.

The true penitent has one object for which he lives and acts, in which he took no interest before. *It is, that all men may become Christians.*

He sees that this is the object for which Christ came into the world, and that God will be honored, and all men made happy, by its accomplishment.

He sees that if the Bible were given to all men, and if all would love and obey it, this world would be a very different world from what it now is. It would be like one great family of brothers and sisters, with Christ at the head of it, all imitating and obeying him, and each one trying to make the rest good and happy.

He wonders and sorrows that he never saw and felt this before. He has been living among Christians, and has known something of what they were doing to build up the kingdom of Christ in the world. He has known about the different societies that were engaged in this good and great work. He has heard of revivals of religion; of the pouring out of the Spirit of God upon the hearts of men; and of sinners being brought to repentance, and to trust in Christ. He has read, perhaps, of what mission-aries are doing in other lands; and how the hea-then are giving up their idols and false religions, and becoming worshippers of the true God, and friends of the Redeemer.

He sees now, and feels, what a selfish and sinful heart he has had, that these good, and great, and glorious things have been wholly uninteresting to him. For the best interests and eternal welfare of his fellow-men he has cared not at all.

He mourns over this his selfishness and neglect of duty. He confesses his great guilt to God. He wakes up from his stupidity, to *a life of prayer and activity in the service of the Redeemer.*

He contributes liberally, according to his means, to the different benevolent societies, whose object is to do good to his fellow-men, and to build up the kingdom of Christ in the world. He aids these so-cieties, if he has the ability, by his personal labors. He prays constantly and earnestly for the blessing of God upon them.

He seeks, too, in his own family, and neighborhood, and circle of friends, and the place where he lives, to lead sinners to Jesus Christ. He finds opportunities of talking with them about what they must do to be saved, and of urging them to repent, and trust in the Savior. He remembers them, daily, in his prayers, beseeching God to give them his Holy Spirit, and to lead them to love and obey him.

He endeavors, also, in one other important way, to build up the kingdom of Christ in the hearts of all around him, *by his example.*

He endeavors to show that he has the spirit of Christ, and that he desires to do good to others, by being kind and generous to them in little things, in the daily intercourse and business of life. He takes very great pains to be frank, honest, and upright in all his dealings, *willing rather to give others the advantage than to take it himself,* and most conscientiously doing to others as he would have others do to him.

He is ready to help the poor, to visit the sick, to be a friend of the friendless, and to contribute to the comfort, and improvement, and innocent enjoyment of his fellow-men in this world.

Unless repentance is accompanied, in a greater or less degree, with these effects upon the heart and the conduct, it cannot be of the right kind. This desire to do good as he has opportunity, and to extend the blessings of the Gospel of Christ among his fellow-men, will show itself in the sincere penitent.

The longer he lives, the more it will show itself, the more in this respect he will be like Christ, who, while on earth, gave up every thing else, that he might do the will of God, in doing good to the bodies and to the souls of men.

And, my dear children, if you truly repent of your sins, you will feel this same desire. You will wish and pray, that the kingdom of Christ may be built up throughout the world. You will *act*, too, as you are able to understand what you ought to do, and according to the means which you have of doing it. You will try to do good to others, that they may see that you have the spirit of Christ, and that they may be led, *by your example*, to trust in this Savior, and love and obey him.

If one of you should tell me that you hoped you had repented of sin, and I should see, notwithstanding, that you took no interest in building up *the kingdom of Christ in our own family*, I should think you were greatly deceived.

A true penitent, deeply sorry for his own sins, and grateful to God, above all things, that *he has found a Savior*, and yet caring nothing for the soul of a brother, or sister, or friend; never praying for them, or conversing with them, to try to lead them to Christ! What an absurdity!

Think of this, my children, and let it assist you to judge correctly of what true repentance is.

CHAPTER XV.

He who begins to repent will keep on repenting. He will look to the Holy Spirit to aid and strengthen him in loving and serving God. He will rely entirely on what Christ did and suffered, for forgiveness and acceptance with God.

Mother. We are now, my children, drawing near the conclusion of our subject. I am glad to see that you have been so attentive. Give me this attention a little longer.

William. I should think, mother, from all that you have told us, a person must go on repenting during his whole life.

Mother. He who *begins* truly to repent of his sins, will *keep on* repenting so long as he has any sin left. For there is as much reason that he should do this at one time as at another. Sin is always offen-sive to God, in those who have any love and obedience to him, as well as in those who have none; in small things as well as in great.

Some seem to think that repentance is a work to be done all at once, or in a very short time; and that, after having felt *sorry enough* for their sins, they never need feel sorry again.

You, children, can see what a great mistake this is. If one of you had disobeyed me yesterday, and should now feel truly sorry for it, and ask my forgiveness, is that a reason why you need not feel sorry again to-morrow, and ask my forgiveness, if you should again disobey me?

No, no; the true penitent is the very person to be the most ready to mourn over his sins, if he commits any. For he knows and feels how great an evil sin is. And the mercy which God has shown him, through Christ, in pardoning his past sins,—this wonderful love of God, and of the Savior,—will melt him into the deepest sorrow, when he finds that he has yielded to temptation and sinned against such goodness and compassion.

He will feel, too, *how liable he is to sin.*

This is another mark of true repentance. The true penitent knows that if God had left him to himself, he would have gone on to sin more and more. He would have become more and more hardened in sin. He would have kept on in the way to eternal ruin.

He knows that it was the Holy Spirit which opened his eyes, the eyes of his mind, to see his guilt and danger, and that it was the same Spirit which led him, by *an almighty power and influence*, to turn unto God, to repent of his sins, and to trust in the Lord Jesus Christ. He feels that it is the same Spirit which must aid and strengthen him in doing his duty as a faithful follower of the Redeemer.

He feels that, although he must strive, himself, to overcome all sin, and to resist all temptation, his own strength is weakness. He says, as Paul did, " I can do all things through Christ, which strengtheneth me."

He prays continually for *this divine aid*. He feels his dependence on God; and when he begins to feel strong in himself, and to forget his dependence on God, he finds that then is the very time that temptation has its greatest power, and that he is in the greatest danger of falling into sin.

He learns wisdom from this, and the longer he lives, the more earnest his constant prayer is, that *he may be strengthened, with might, by the Spirit of God, in the inner man*—in all the holy thoughts, feelings, desires, and purposes of his soul.

He remembers, too, the promises of God, under all his trials and temptations.

"They that wait upon the Lord shall renew their strength."

"Fear thou not, for I am with thee. Be not dismayed, for I am thy God. I will strengthen thee: yea, I will help thee; yea, I will uphold thee with the right hand of my righteousness."

The last thing which I shall mention as always accompanying true repentance, is *an entire reliance on what Christ did and suffered for the forgiveness of sin, and for acceptance with God.*

The true penitent feels that he cannot, by his repentance, make any reparation to God for his past sins. If he is forgiven, he knows that it must be through the mercy of God. He cannot ask for forgiveness *as a right*, or because, by repenting, he has done something which entitles him to forgiveness. He cannot ask for it as what *he deserves*, on account of his being so good in repenting of his sins. For repenting is just what he ought to do, even if he were to receive no favor whatever from God; yes, even if he were to be punished for his sins, to the full extent of what God has threatened.

If a man has done something very wrong, if he has stolen, or murdered some one, and suffers the punishment which the laws threaten against such an offence, ought he not still to be truly sorry for it?

Sometimes, my children, you know, I have been obliged to punish you for doing wrong, although you seemed to be very sorry for it, and promised never to do so again. Your being sorry did not entitle you to be freed from the punishment, or make it wrong or unjust in me to inflict it. Your being sorry did not even make it *unkind* in me to punish you.

I might have seen that *the good of the family* rendered it absolutely necessary that you should be punished, notwithstanding your sorrow and promise of amendment.

If I have at any time forgiven you, it has been an act of mercy towards you. Your being sorry did not give you a right to demand forgiveness, or to ask for it, as something which you deserved.

The forgiveness of our sins, on the part of God, is in him *an act of mere mercy.* If he had not shown sinners this mercy, we should have had no right to complain.

You have no right to complain, if, when you do wrong, I punish you. I may see, that the good of the family requires it.

If God had concluded that *the good of his great family,* of the whole collection of beings whom he has formed, required the punishment of all who break his laws, without any forgiveness, without any mercy, we could never complain that this was unjust or unkind on his part.

But he has found out a way in which he can be just, and preserve the authority of his government, and yet show us mercy.

HIS SON, JESUS CHRIST, DIED ON THE CROSS.

On account of his death, God can now forgive our sins. He tells us so in the Bible, and he tells us that if we believe what he says, and feel truly sorry for our sins, and trust in Christ as our only Savior, *he will forgive us.*

God also assures us that this is *the only way* in which he will show us mercy.

He has very important reasons for saying so. His wisdom, his justice, his holiness, his goodness require that he should show us mercy only in this way.

Now, if we know all this, and if God also *commands us* to believe on the Lord Jesus Christ, that we may be saved; you see, my children, that you cannot truly repent of your sins without at the same time trusting in Christ as your only Savior. How can you be truly sorry for your other acts of disobedience against God and resistance of his authority, if you do not obey his command and submit to his authority in this particular?

I have gone into this explanation that I might fix

it in your minds, never to be forgotten, *that you cannot truly repent of your sins without trusting entirely in Christ for the forgiveness of your sins, and your acceptance with God.*

The true penitent always thus trusts in Christ. His knowledge of the evil of sin shows him that such a Savior is necessary. And, on the other hand, the death of this Savior shows him how great an evil sin is.

His feeling of guilt leads him to see how much *he needs* such a Savior; and, on the other hand, the death of this Savior shows him the greatness of his guilt.

His most ungrateful sin, that which has shown most clearly the pride and obstinacy of his heart, has been his rejection of this Savior, his utter unwillingness to trust in him. How can he feel any true repentance without repenting of *this sin?* How can he repent of this sin without going to the Savior whom he has so long rejected, and trusting in him with all his heart?

He does thus trust in him. The same spirit of obedience, of submission, and of love to God, which shows itself in *his repentance* for his sins, shows itself in *his faith* in the Redeemer. They go together. The stronger the one is, the stronger the other will be.

They continue together in the breast of every one who has truly turned from sin, to love and obey God

The sorrow of the true penitent led him to Christ. It led him to this Savior, that in this way he might show his love to God and obedience to his authority.

It led him to this Savior, that in this way he might show his gratitude for such rich mercy.

It led him to this Savior, that in this way he might obtain the forgiveness of his sins, and a deliverance from them.

The same sorrow for *his remaining sins* leads the true penitent continually to look unto Christ. For he knows that it is only for his sake, and through him, that he can receive *divine aid* to carry him through the duties, the trials, and the temptations of life.

He can do all things, through Christ strengthening him.

He began with trusting in Christ, when he first became a child of God. He keeps near to Christ during the whole course of his journey to heaven. He hopes to meet death in peace, because Christ will be with him; and then to enjoy the more immediate presence and love of this Savior, in that holy and happy world where he has gone to prepare a place for all his followers.

CHAPTER XVI.

How long does it take a person to repent? What keeps the sinner from repenting?

Mother. I am thankful to God, my dear children, that I have had so good an opportunity of explaining to you, in our late conversations, what true repentance is.

You may have thought that it would be a great deal more pleasant to you, to hear some amusing story of the same length. But I cannot but hope you will feel quite satisfied with what I have done. It is very important, while young persons and children have so much to amuse them, and especially while so many books of mere entertainment are put into their hands, that they should be required, also, to attend to subjects of a serious kind, and to understand which, patient thought is necessary.

You cannot improve your minds, or gain useful knowledge, without thinking, and *thinking hard* sometimes.

You cannot gain religious knowledge by merely reading stories that have some religious truth in them.

You must be willing to be patient and attentive

ın learning religious truth, to think about it, to study it, to make efforts to understand it.

These are some of the reasons why I have talked so long with you on the subject of repentance.

I think you must have seen that it requires much care and thought in the person who attempts to explain it, and also great attention and close thinking in those who are learning about it.

I hope neither my labor nor your attention will be lost. I know indeed that my instructions will do you no good, unless God accompanies them with the influences of his Holy Spirit upon your minds, and upon your hearts. O may he give you all the Holy Spirit, that you may get good from what I have been teaching you——that you may truly repent of your sins, and trust in the Lord Jesus Christ.

William. Yesterday, mother, we children were together in the parlor, and Edward asked me *how long it would take a person to repent.* I told him I did not know. Eliza said she thought it would take a long time for any body to have all the thoughts and feelings which you have been explaining to us. I thought so too; and as we were all rather in trouble about it, we agreed that we would ask you the question this evening.

Mother. I am glad, my children, that you have

thought of asking me this question. I will endeavor to answer it.

I do not suppose that you must have precisely all the thoughts and feelings which I have been describing to you, in order that *you may know, by feeling it, what true repentance is.*

But you must have *the temper of mind*—(*the kind of feelings* towards God, and towards Christ) —which if you *begin to have it* will lead you sooner or later to have *all the thoughts and feelings* which I have described. I mean, if your life is spared, and if you do what you ought, to find out what your duty is. But if you do not use the means; such as studying the Bible; and attending public worship; and reading good books; and conversing with wise and pious persons; and examining your own hearts and conduct; and praying to God for the Holy Spirit to teach and guide you; if you are not faithful in the use of these means, then you will have great reason to doubt whether you have ever known, by feeling it, what true repentance is.

With this explanation, unless you sooner or later have all the thoughts and feelings which I have been describing to you in our late conversations, you cannot hope that you have truly repented of your sins, and trusted in the Lord Jesus Christ.

You may not have these thoughts and feelings

in the same order in which I have described them.
You may not have them in the same degree, or with
the same clearness and strength. You may sometimes fail to have them at all, by yielding to temptation, and falling into sin.

But you will have *so much* of them as to know
what they are by *your own experience;* that is, by
having these thoughts and feelings in your own
soul, and by seeing how they make you *more like
Christ in your conversation and conduct.*

You will keep on having *more and more of them,*
as you grow older; and unless this is the case, it is
certain that you have never, never known, by feeling
it, any thing of what true repentance is.

Edward. I think I understand, mother, all that
you have just been saying. Still you have not told
us how long it takes a person to repent.

Mother. Have a little patience, my son. I was
preparing to answer the question, which I will now
attempt to do.

Do you remember, Edward, how much out of
temper you were yesterday morning, when you were
pulling the book away from Eliza?

Edward. I do, mother, and I think I feel sorry
for it.

Eliza. I never saw him so angry before. I was al
most afraid he was going to strike me.

Mother. Did you hear me, Edward, when I first told you to let the book entirely alone?

Edward. I do not know, mother.

William. I do not think he did. He was in such a rage, and pulling the book so hard, that he seemed not to hear you.

Edward. But I began to hear you pretty soon, mother, though I did not understand at first exactly what you said.

Mother. What did you hear me say, when you did understand me?

Edward. I forgot about the book a moment. I listened to what you said. I heard you say, "Edward, let that book entirely alone."

Mother. Did you hear me say immediately after —"you ought to be ashamed and sorry for such conduct, and if you repeat it again, I must punish you?"

Edward. I did, mother.

Mother. How long did it take you to stop pulling the book, and to feel that you ought to obey me, and be sorry for what you had done?

Edward. Just as long as I was stopping to listen to what you were saying, and thinking what I ought to do, and feeling that it was best not to pull the book any more.

Mother. You ought, in the same way, to stop and think what your guilt, your danger, and your duty are, and to feel true repentance towards God for all your sins, and to trust in the Lord Jesus Christ for the forgiveness of your sins, and for acceptance with God. How long would it take you to do this?

Edward. I suppose, if I felt right, mother, I could do it very soon.

Mother. Well, you have answered your own question. If a person understands what it is to repent, and feels right towards God, he can repent very soon.

He is truly sorry for all his past sins. He desires to forsake them. He hates them, as committed against a holy, just, and good God. He looks to the mercy of God, through Christ, for pardon. He trusts in this Savior. He looks to the Holy Spirit to teach him, to aid him, and to strengthen him; and with a fixed purpose of soul resolves in future to love and obey God.

Now, just so long as it takes to have these thoughts and feelings, does it take a person to feel true repentance in his heart.

It takes a longer time, no doubt, for him to understand what true repentance is, if he has never had it explained to him.

If a little child should come into our family from some heathen country, who knew nothing about God and the Savior, you know I should have to spend some time in teaching him what the duty of repentance towards God and faith in the Lord Jesus Christ is.

But, after he understood what it is, although he might not understand it as well as you do, I might say to him, "you ought *now* to repent of all your sins, and trust in Christ;" and if he felt right towards God, it would not take him long to do it.

Why do not *you*, my dear children, *begin* to feel right towards God; to be truly sorry for your sins; and trusting in Christ, and looking to the Holy Spirit for aid and strength, resolve—feel willing and determined in your soul—that you will love and obey God in future ?

Why do you not begin to do it this day, this evening—*now ?*

William. There is something in me, mother, that keeps me from doing it.

Eliza. And so there is in me, mother.

Edward. And in me.

Mother. Ah ! my children, what is that *something in you* which keeps you from loving and serving such a great and good Being as God is, and from trusting in such a kind and compassionate Savior as is the Lord Jesus Christ ?

It is your own selfish and wicked feelings and desires.

You love yourself, and seek your own good, without desiring and trying to make others good and happy. You would have their happiness lessened, or even destroyed, when it interferes with your own comfort or enjoyment. You love other things more than you love God, while you know that you ought to love him with your whole soul, and to love others as you do yourself. You do *not like* his commands. You do not feel willing *to submit entirely* to his authority.

You are *unwilling* therefore to humble yourself before him, to repent, to turn unto God, and to seek his mercy through Christ.

It is all nothing more than your own selfish and wicked feelings and desires.

I speak very plainly to you, my children. It is my duty to do so. I wish to have you feel your guilt and your danger. Think of what we have been talking about this evening. Think of it when you go alone to pray to God.

CHAPTER XVII.

May the sinner pray for the Holy Spirit? How is it that the Holy Spirit leads the sinner to repentance, and yet that his repentance is his own act? The sinner urged to repent.

Mother. Well, my children, what do you think of our last conversation?

Edward. I do not know what to do, mother.

Eliza. I hope I shall repent and trust in Christ, before I die.

William. I wish to ask a question about it.

Mother. Do so, my son; you know I am always happy to have you ask me questions, and to answer them, if it is in my power.

William. Is it right, mother, for me to pray to God for the Holy Spirit to help me to repent?

Mother. Let us see if it is. Your own selfish and wicked feelings and desires, as we have seen, keep you from repenting. You are to blame for having such feelings and desires. You are very guilty in having them. You are in great danger. You are justly condemned by the law of God for not loving him with your whole soul, and for not loving others as you do yourself.

Your guilt, too, is increased by your not being

sorry for all this, and by your not accepting of God's offers of mercy through Christ.

If God should leave you to go on in sin, and to die impenitent, and to be miserable for ever, you could not accuse him of not treating you as you deserved.

For he is ready to receive you *now*, if you will go to him, repenting of your sins and trusting in Christ. You do not choose to go in this way. *You are unwilling to go.*

If you receive, then, the punishment which your sins deserve, you can blame no one but yourself.

What is to be done? You must repent, and trust in Christ, or you cannot be saved. You must do this *yourself*. It must be *your own* repenting, and *your own* trusting in Christ. *You* must do it. If any one else does it, it will not be *your doing it.*

Alas! your selfish and wicked feelings and desires keep you from doing it.

You acknowledge all this, and you feel yourself to be a poor, lost, sinful, helpless being.

You *are* so; and unless God has mercy on you, there is no hope in your case. He is not bound to help you. *But he may help you.* His Holy Spirit alone can overcome your unwillingness to repent and trust in Christ. *He may give you this Holy Spirit.* He has given it to others, as poor, lost, and sinful as you are. His compassion and mercy are very great.

It is *his* kind providence which has given you a mother, and permitted you to hear her explain your duty to you.

It is *his* Holy Spirit which has awakened your conscience to think at all of your guilt and danger, and has led you to desire to pray to him.

Yes, my son, go to God, and pray for his Holy Spirit. Your very prayer may be the means of leading you to see, and to feel, more strongly, your guilt and your danger.

Yes; go to God, and pray for his Holy Spirit. When can you be in a better situation to repent of sin, and to trust in the Lord Jesus Christ, than while praying to God?

Yes; go to God, and pray for his Holy Spirit. While going, while bowing down before him, while pouring out your cries for mercy, the Holy Spirit may *already be given to you*, and you may find *yourself willing* to submit to the authority of God; repenting of all your disobedience and ingratitude towards him, and trusting in Jesus Christ as your only Savior and hope.

But remember that your praying has nothing in it to make you deserving of any favor from God. If he has mercy on you, it will not be on account of any thing good which he sees in you. It will be because he chooses to have mercy on you on account of what Christ did and suffered.

Remember, also, that whatever else you may do, God has declared that unless you repent of your sins and trust in Christ, you cannot be saved.

William. One thing still troubles me, mother, in thinking on this subject.

Mother. What is that, my son?

William. You have told us that *the Holy Spirit alone can overcome our unwillingness to repent and trust in Christ.*

How then can *I* do any thing? The Holy Spirit must lead me to repent. I shall not alone, of myself, repent. I must wait till God gives me his Holy Spirit; and he will do this when he thinks best.

Mother. I will not say, my son, that there is no difficulty in this. I will not say that I am able fully to explain it.

I see difficulties in many other subjects, which, nevertheless, do not prevent my believing and my acting.

It is God who causes the corn to grow; and yet it will not grow unless man plants it and hoes it.

It is God who causes the wind to blow, and fill the sails of a ship, so as to conduct it across the ocean; and yet the captain and the sailors must do a great deal, or the ship would never reach the place of its destination.

It is God who keeps us in life every day. "In him we live, and move, and have our being." But we must do many things in the way of preserving our lives, or we should soon die.

It is the Holy Spirit alone which can overcome your unwillingness to repent and trust in Christ, and yet you must *do* these things yourself.

How the Holy Spirit acts, and yet leads you to act, so that the repenting of sin and the trusting in Christ are truly your own acts, I am not able to explain. In some way the Holy Spirit *makes you willing*.

Suppose that, by disobeying the directions of your father, you had wandered away, and got into a very difficult and dangerous path.

You are on the edge of a steep precipice, and a few more steps will sink you into a dreadful gulf beneath.

There is *one way* of escape, a kind voice from above tells you so, but you are unwilling to take it. It is a narrow and difficult way. It looks forbidding. You dislike it utterly.

It is your father who calls to you. He persuades you to enter upon the path of safety. He stretches out his arm to aid you. He tells you you will be lost if you do not grasp his hand, and cling to it strong ly, and rely on his strength. He tells you, you will be lost if you do not put forth all your own strength, and make all the effort in your power. He makes you willing to take the path of safety. You choose freely to take it. He acts, and you act, and you are rescued from ruin.

He might have left you to the destruction that would be the just consequence of your disobedience. He might not have spoken to you, or stretched out his arm to save you. Then you would have perish-ed. He had compassion on you. He saved you ; and yet you would not have been saved if you had not yourself been *willing to act*, if you had not yourself *acted*.

Now, I do not say that this is exactly like what your case would be if you were made willing, by the Holy Spirit, to repent of your sins, and to trust in Christ. The *manner* in which the Holy Spirit does this cannot be explained. We only know that it is in some way which does not destroy your free agen-cy, which leaves the repenting of sin, and the trust-ing in Christ, to be *your own act*, and which, notwith-standing, makes it sure that you will do these things.

Be thankful, my child, that *it is so*. Do not trou-ble yourself with the difficulties of explaining *how* it is so.

Go to your heavenly Father. Do you feel the least disposition to go? It is the Holy Spirit which is already granting you his aid. Feel your dependence on this aid. Look above for strength. Put forth your own strength. Go to your heavenly Father. Pour out your soul before him. Confess your sins to him. Pray for the Holy Spirit. Pray that you may be led to repent and trust in Christ. Repent and trust in this Savior, and you shall find peace and joy.

I say these things to you all, my dear children. Think of them as you retire. Good night.

CHAPTER XVIII.

Expostulation with the impenitent reader.

We have done with the conversations between Mrs. Dormer and her children. The author would indulge the hope that, with the Divine blessing, they may do good to the reader, or to those who have heard them read.

Can it be that any one, either younger or older, has gone through with them, and yet feels little or no anxiety on the subject of *repentance towards God, and faith in the Lord Jesus Christ?*

If any such person is still listening to what the author has to say, may he be permitted, before concluding the book, to present a few more thoughts for the consideration of the reader?

My friend, do you not think that the description which has been given of sin is a true one? Is it not a great evil, *wrong in itself*, as committed against the greatest, the wisest, and the best of Beings—against one who has *a perfect right* to the love and obedience of all his creatures? Will you go on refusing to yield to God what is his just due?

Is not sin a great evil, because it opposes the government and authority of God, which are absolutely necessary to the order and happiness of the great family of beings whom he has formed, and of which he is the head? Can you go on in sin without showing that *you care nothing for the real happiness of your fellow beings?* Are you willing to continue adding and adding to the guilt of such wicked selfishness?

Is not sin a great evil, because it shows such *vile ingratitude* towards that Being who has given you so many blessings and privileges? Think, too, of his great forbearance and long-suffering, in sparing your life, while you have been so disobedient and ungrateful to him. Think of his amazing love, in sending his only and well-beloved Son to pour out his blood on the cross, that a way might be opened for your pardon and safety. Think of the tender pity, the wonderful kindness of this Savior towards you. Will you go on in this vile ingratitude against such a merciful Father, against such a compassionate Redeemer?

Is not sin a great evil, because it opposes and is continually breaking *two commands of God*, which he has given us that his honor and government might be preserved, and our own true happiness secured, both in this world and the world to come?

These commands, if obeyed, will lead to the obedience of all his other commands. They are, as you know, very simple and very plain. If you are a child you can understand them.

Thou shalt love the Lord thy God, with all thy heart, and with all thy soul, and with all thy strength, and with all thy mind, and thy neighbor as thyself.

Are not these commands reasonable? Are they not right in all respects? Think as much as you choose, and see if you can find any fault with them. In what way would you have them altered that they may be made better?

Do you not see that *the spirit of love, and of submission to rightful authority*, which these commands require, is absolutely necessary to our comfort and happiness, even in this world? Must you not admit, without a single doubt, that if all persons obeyed these two commands, we should have very happy and delightful families, and neighborhoods, and towns, and cities, and countries, and that the whole earth would begin to be like heaven?

Is not the disobedience of these two commands of God the cause of all the wickedness, and misery, and suffering that exist in the world? Is not the violation of them a very great evil? How great must be your guilt in having lived thus far in the constant violation of these commands!

Is not sin a great evil, because it debases the soul, and makes it feel, if it has any conscience left, that it is low and mean in sinning? Yes, my friend, if you have any conscience, you must feel that sin is mean and low in itself, that it sinks the sinner in his own opinion of himself, and that God and the Savior, and all pure and holy beings, must look on his sins with loathing and abhorrence. You must feel, and I dare say you have often felt so, in looking upon *real Christians*, (I do not mean pretended ones,) that in forsaking sin, and in loving and serving God, and devoting themselves to doing good to their fellow-men, they were taking altogether the best course. You have felt, and still feel, that theirs is the course, not only of safety and duty, but of true wisdom and of the highest honor. *Is not sin a great evil*, because it keeps you from taking this course, and makes you loathe and despise yourself, while you are sinning against God?

Is not sin a great evil, because, if not repented of, and pardoned through the mercy of God in Christ, it will make the soul wretched and miserable for ever?

Think, my friend, of your never-dying soul. It is to live for ever—for years and ages of which you can form no idea.

If all the houses in the place where you live were filled with fine sand, and you should begin at one house to carry out the sand, as ants do, one grain at a time, and carry it away five hundred miles, and then come back after another grain, and so on till the house was emptied, how long would it take you to do it, if God should let you live so long? The number of years would be so great that you cannot think how great it would be.

Suppose your life should continue, and you should keep on in the same way till you had emptied all the houses of the sand. How long would it take?

Now suppose there was a round globe, as big as our earth is, composed of grains of fine sand, all of which were to be carried away, one by one, in the same manner.

Suppose, still farther, that there were hundreds,

thousands, millions of such globes of sand, and that millions of years were taken in carrying away a single grain. How many years would it take to carry them all away? The mind is lost and bewildered in trying to think about it.

But the soul will live all this number of years, and then only, as it were, *just begin to live.* It will keep on living as great a number of years again and again, thousands and millions of times over, and then keep on living, and keep on and never stop living. *The soul will live for ever.*

What is the amount of the happiness, or the misery, which the soul will enjoy or suffer during its never-ending existence in the future world? You can form no idea of it. It will be as much greater than what you can enjoy or suffer in this world, as your eternal existence will be longer than the few short years of your life on this side of the grave! You cannot think, then, how much the soul is worth. What would it profit you, if you should gain all the pleasures, the riches, and the honors of this world, and yet *lose your soul;* be banished, from the presence of God and the Savior, and all holy and happy beings, and be sentenced to dwell in wretchedness for ever, with beings as sinful and as miserable as yourself!

Sin, if not repented of, and pardoned by the mercy

of God, through Christ, will cause all this evil to .he soul—*to your soul.*

God has told us so, in the Bible. His words are everlasting truth. He cannot deceive us. He has declared his purpose, and he will not change.

" God so loved the world, that he gave his only begotten Son, that whosoever believeth in him should not perish, but have everlasting life."

" He that believeth on the Son, hath everlasting life; and he that believeth not the Son, shall not see life: but *the wrath of God abideth on him.*"

How terrible must be the wrath of so pure and holy, so just and good a being as God is! And this wrath *to abide* on the soul, to continue as long as the soul lives! My friend, can you dare to die impenitent, and to have this wrath abide on *you?* Can you venture to continue in impenitence any longer, while life is so uncertain, and God may call you into eternity any moment?

Is not sin a great evil, which can thus ruin the soul for ever? Is it not *to you* a great evil, since by it you are *now exposed* to this ruin, and must certainly fall into it, if you do not repent of your sins, and trust in Christ?

Do you begin to see something of the evil of sin? Ah! you see it yet very indistinctly. If you could see it as God sees it, in its true and awful character, you would soon be in great alarm at your guilt and danger.

Try, my friend, try to get clearer and more affecting views of the evil of sin, and of your own extreme sinfulness in the sight of a holy and just God. Think over what you have been reading in this book. Meditate upon it seriously, and in retirement.

Read, too, the Bible. There you will see the evil of sin. There you will see how God abhors sin. There you will see the amazing love of Christ in dying to save you from sin, and its dreadful consequences. There you will find every motive that can be thought of to lead you to repentance, and to trust in Christ. There you are warned by all the terrors of eternal wo, to flee from the wrath to come. There you are invited by all the joys of heaven, to accept of the mercy of God, and to be prepared for endless holiness and happiness beyond the grave.

Will you not begin this day, this hour, *now*, to give your serious attention to this all important subject? Will you not go alone, and take your Bible with you, and read it, and think of the things which concern the eternal welfare of your soul?

What hinders your doing this? What hinders your going immediately to God, and pouring out your soul before him in humble confession of your sins; deeply penitent for your guilt; imploring his mercy through Christ; and praying for the influences of the Holy Spirit, that you may be led to begin a life of love and obedience to God, and of devotedness to his service?

Have you any desire, however faint, to do this? O yield to it. The Spirit of Grace is drawing you to Christ. Will you resist this Spirit? Will you grieve this Spirit to depart from you, and leave you to greater blindness of mind and hardness of heart? Will you give up all hopes of becoming the friend of God, and of having an interest in Christ? Will you go back to your course of sin and guilt, and hazard the eternal loss of your soul?

THE END.

Other Related SGCB Titles

In addition to *The Child's Book on Repentance* Solid Ground is honored to offer a full dozen other uncovered treasure for children and young people.

The Child's Book on the Fall by Thomas H. Gallaudet is a simple and practical exposition of the Fall of man into sin, and his only hope of salvation.

Repentance & Faith: *Explained and Illustrated for the Young* by Charles Walker, is a two in one book introducing children to the difference between true and false faith and repentance.

The Child at Home by John S.C. Abbott is the sequel to his popular book *The Mother at Home.* A must read for children and their parents.

My Brother's Keeper: *Letters to a Younger Brother* by J.W. Alexander contains the actual letters Alexander sent to his ten year old brother.

The Scripture Guide by J.W. Alexander is filled with page after page of information on getting the most from our Bibles. Invaluable!

Feed My Lambs: *Lectures to Children* by John Todd is drawn from actual sermons preached in Philadelphia, PA and Pittsfield, MA to the children of the church, one Sunday each month. A pure gold-mine of instruction.

Heroes of the Reformation by Richard Newton is a unique volume that introduces children and young people to the leading figures and incidents of the Reformation. Spurgeon called him, *"The Prince of preachers to the young."*

Heroes of the Early Church by Richard Newton is the sequel to the above-named volume. The very last book Newton wrote introduces all the leading figures of the early church with lessons to be learned from each figure.

The King's Highway: *Ten Commandments to the Young* by Richard Newton is a volume of Newton's sermons to children. Highly recommended!

The Life of Jesus Christ for the Young by Richard Newton is a double volume set that traces the Gospel from Genesis 3:15 to the Ascension of our Lord and the outpouring of His Spirit on the Day of Pentecost. Excellent!

The Young Lady's Guide by Harvey Newcomb will speak directly to the heart of the young women who desire to serve Christ with all their being.

The Chief End of Man by John Hall is an exposition and application of the first question of the Westminster Shorter Catechism. Full of rich illustrations.

Call us Toll Free at 1-877-666-9469
Send us an e-mail at sgcb@charter.net
Visit us on line at solid-ground-books.com

Other Solid Ground Titles

THE COMMUNICANT'S COMPANION by *Matthew Henry*

THE SECRET OF COMMUNION WITH GOD by *Matthew Henry*

THE MOTHER AT HOME by *John S.C. Abbott*

LECTURES ON THE ACTS OF THE APOSTLES *by John Dick*

THE FORGOTTEN HEROES OF LIBERTY by *J.T. Headley*

LET THE CANNON BLAZE AWAY by *Joseph P. Thompson*

THE STILL HOUR: *Communion with God in Prayer* by *Austin Phelps*

COLLECTED WORKS of James Henley Thornwell (4 vols.)

CALVINISM IN HISTORY *by Nathaniel S. McFetridge*

OPENING SCRIPTURE: *Hermeneutical Manual by Patrick Fairbairn*

THE ASSURANCE OF FAITH *by Louis Berkhof*

THE PASTOR IN THE SICK ROOM *by John D. Wells*

THE BUNYAN OF BROOKLYN: *Life & Sermons of I.S. Spencer*

THE NATIONAL PREACHER: *Sermons from 2nd Great Awakening*

FIRST THINGS: *First Lessons God Taught Mankind Gardiner Spring*

BIBLICAL & THEOLOGICAL STUDIES *by 1912 Faculty of Princeton*

THE POWER OF GOD UNTO SALVATION *by B.B. Warfield*

THE LORD OF GLORY *by B.B. Warfield*

A GENTLEMAN & A SCHOLAR: *Memoir of J.P. Boyce by J. Broadus*

SERMONS TO THE NATURAL MAN *by W.G.T. Shedd*

SERMONS TO THE SPIRITUAL MAN *by W.G.T. Shedd*

HOMILETICS AND PASTORAL THEOLOGY *by W.G.T. Shedd*

A PASTOR'S SKETCHES 1 & 2 *by Ichabod S. Spencer*

THE PREACHER AND HIS MODELS *by James Stalker*

IMAGO CHRISTI: *The Example of Jesus Christ by James Stalker*

LECTURES ON THE HISTORY OF PREACHING *by J. A. Broadus*

THE SHORTER CATECHISM ILLUSTRATED *by John Whitecross*

THE CHURCH MEMBER'S GUIDE *by John Angell James*

THE SUNDAY SCHOOL TEACHER'S GUIDE *by John A. James*

CHRIST IN SONG: *Hymns of Immanuel from All Ages* by *Philip Schaff*

DEVOTIONAL LIFE OF THE S.S. TEACHER *by J.R. Miller*

Call us Toll Free at 1-877-666-9469
Send us an e-mail at sgcb@charter.net
Visit us on line at solid-ground-books.com

CPSIA information can be obtained
at www.ICGtesting.com
Printed in the USA
BVHW030337260821
614918BV00001B/46